DISCOVER
GALATIANS

Freedom in Christ

LEADER GUIDE

Thank you to Tamara Veenstra Shreur for the original version. Thank you to Sharon Hurlds, Cheryl Dion, Christine Dykstra, Joy Sharpe, and Gillian Ferwerda for the revision. Thank you to Dr. Jeff Sajdak from Calvin Theological Seminary for the theological review.

Unless otherwise noted, Scripture quotations are from the HOLY BIBLE, NEW INTERNATIONAL VERSION®, NIV® Copyright © 1973, 1978, 1984, 2011 by Biblica, Inc.™ Used by permission.
All rights reserved worldwide.

Discover Your Bible series. *Discover Galatians* (Leader Guide), © 2022, 1986 by Faith Alive Christian Resources, 1700 28th Street SE, Grand Rapids, MI 49508-1407. All rights reserved. With the exception of brief excerpts for review purposes, no part of this book may be reproduced in any manner whatsoever without written permission from the publisher. For information or questions about use of copyrighted material please contact Permissions, Faith Alive Christian Resources, 1700 28th Street SE, Grand Rapids, MI 49508-1407; phone: 1-800-333-8300; e-mail: permissions@faithaliveresources.org.

We welcome your comments. Call us at 1-800-272-5125 or e-mail us at info@DiscoverYourBible.org.

ISBN 978-1-56212-604-9

5 4 3 2 1

Contents

To the Leader..4

Introduction 9

Historical Snapshot...10

God's Story..13

Map...14

Glossary of Terms 15

Lesson 1: A Different Gospel 21

Lesson 2: Defending the Faith...33

Lesson 3: Faith or Law..44

Lesson 4: Sons, Not Slaves!..55

Lesson 5: A Pastor's Plea..67

Lesson 6: Set Free in Christ..79

Lesson 7: Life in the Spirit 90

Lesson 8: A Brief Benediction 102

Lesson 9: Truly Free!..111

Invitation and Prayer of Commitment 119

Bibliography...121

Evaluation

To the Leader

The Role of a Bible Discovery Leader

What role do you have as a Bible study small group leader?

I am not...	I am...

Bible discovery leaders are not teachers but guides, facilitators, and conversation leaders. Bible discovery leaders help people discover together what the Bible says and means.

Write your mission in your own words:

Preparing the Lesson

How do you prepare?

- Allow God to speak to *you* through his Word.
- Answer the Study Guide questions yourself first.
- Ask your own questions of the Bible passage. Write these down.
- Then use the Leader Guide to enrich your understanding of the passage.
- Prepare well! Do not bring your Leader Guide to the Bible study group meeting. You do not want to give the impression that the Leader Guide is an answer book. The answers are in the Bible; you are a guide to help your group find the answers in God's Word.

Learn to think in terms of questions. As you prepare, ask yourself questions and try to discover the answers yourself. This will prepare you to anticipate group members' questions and thus help others discover truths from God's Word.

Remember the important questions:

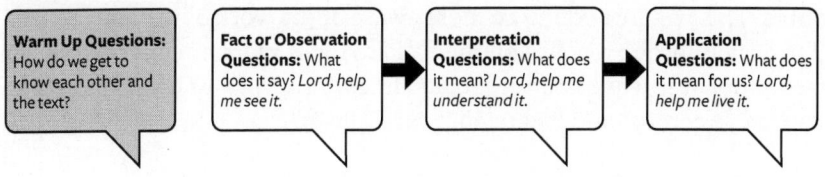

Add questions specifically for your group: You know the interests, personalities, and needs of your group members. You know what they will be curious about or when they will want to dig deeper into a Scripture passage. Put those extra conversation-building questions in your Study Guide and use them during your group time to help get dialogue started. *Do not bring up information simply because you find it interesting.* Know what your group needs, and listen what the Holy Spirit is laying on their hearts!

What do you already know about your group? What might they be curious about?

The text of the Leader Guide includes many extra questions that you may wish to use. Write these in your own Study Guide as well. *You DO NOT have to use all the extra Leader Guide questions.*

Encourage group members to put their own questions and discoveries in their Study Guides. By doing this, they will also be preparing for the group discussion. You might want to start a group discussion by saying, "What questions do you have? What would you like to talk about together?"

Additional helps for your whole group are in the "Introduction," "Historical Snapshot," "Glossary of Terms," and study notes that are in both the Study Guide and the Leader Guide. This will help your whole group discover together, instead of one person being the expert. The Leader Guide also contains insight from commentaries as a resource for you to help guide the conversation. It is based on the New International Version, but any Bible translation can be used.

If you are able to prepare and pray thoroughly before each group session, you will be able to lead without frequent references to your notes. This will free you to be more aware of the work of the Holy Spirit during your group discussion time and to focus more effectively on your facilitation and leadership responsibilities. You will also be able to keep better eye contact and listen more carefully.

What is one specific thing you will do to prepare well?

Leading with Questions

What else can questions do?

- Use questions to direct the group discussion.
- Draw out positive contributions by asking questions.
- Use smaller questions to break down difficult or unclear questions.
- Respond to wrong or problematic answers with questions.
- Direct focus back to the "big idea" of the text with questions when groups get in a tangent.

Think of a time you have seen questions used well. What did the facilitator do?

Group Dynamics

God knows your group. Ask him to help you know your group! If some people in your group are new to the Bible, make certain that you help to clarify information. Clarify religious terms. Be careful not to use extra background material that may add confusion.

Feel free to delve a bit deeper with groups who may be familiar with the Bible. However, keep in mind the evangelistic purpose of this study and make certain that you are being most sensitive to members who may be new to Bible study and may not yet be believers in Christ.

Should differences of opinion arise, allow members to disagree. Your purpose is not to win arguments or even to defend a particular idea. Allow the Holy Spirit to work in the hearts of your group members.

Describe specific ways your group conversation is welcoming to those who are new to Bible study.

Application

As leader, pray that God will first teach you what he wants you to hear from his Word. Ask God to guide you to ask application questions throughout the lesson when it seems appropriate for your group. Help your group see the connection between the Bible and life. *Keep in mind that the purpose of this study is not to fill minds with facts but to change hearts as we learn what God is teaching us through his Word.*

Take a moment and write a prayer that God will change hearts as you learn together. Where can you put that prayer that you will be reminded to pray it regularly? Are there others you might ask to join you in prayer?

Be careful not to be judgmental of persons who may not yet seem to be applying the truths you encounter together. It is the Holy Spirit's work to apply God's Word to people's hearts. Tactfully let the group know how the Spirit is applying the Word in your own heart and life. Pray faithfully for the Spirit's work in others.

Questions for reflection at the end of each session invite everyone to take some time for personal reflection and optional sharing. Try to offer at least a few minutes for reflection time toward the end of each lesson, and encourage group members to do additional follow-up reflection at home.

Wrap Up

What is one thing that stood out to you from this?

What is one thing you will do differently after reading this?

What is one question you still have?

Stay in Touch!

Visit our online learning space for more training! Learn the art of listening to the Holy Spirit, more tips on preparing a lesson, how to finish the season well, and empowering new leaders!

Feel free to contact our office. We would love to answer questions, pray for you, or celebrate what God is doing in your group! Please share your stories! Email info@DiscoverYourBible.org

Introduction

The letter to the Galatians is a bold statement of faith and freedom. Paul knew a lot was at stake – and responds with passion for the core essentials of faith.

Who wrote this and to whom? Paul is likely the author of this letter. Paul was a follower of Jesus, who had grown up Jewish. He shares some of his journey to know Christ in chapter 1 (see also Acts 26:1-23; 9:1- 22). Paul wrote this letter to the churches of North or South Galatia, in Asia Minor of the Roman Empire. If it is to the southern group, this could include churches he had founded in Pisidian Antioch, Lystra, Derbe, and Iconium (Acts 13-14). Most of the believers there had been converted from pagan religions, though there were also many of Jewish background.

What is Galatians? Galatians is a letter, also called an epistle. Paul wrote it to specific churches in a specific context. This letter would have been passed around and read to small house churches in various cities. His letter has three basic divisions: Paul's defense of his authority as teacher and leader in the church (chapters 1 and 2); Paul's reaffirmation of the Christian's freedom from the law and salvation through faith in Christ (chapters 3 and 4); and the life of freedom in Christ (chapters 5 and 6).

When was Galatians written? Perhaps Paul wrote Galatians around A.D. 47-48, before the Jerusalem Council of Acts 15 (likely around A.D. 48 or 49). We have to be aware of the historical context, and the differences in culture and language as we study it today. However, it is God's Word for today as well (Hebrews 4:12; 2 Timothy 3:16).

Indeed, Paul's letter has much to say to us today. What do we believe God requires for salvation? Are our expectations based on God's Word or are they of our own making? Galatians calls us back to a new dependence on God's grace – his undeserved but freely given forgiveness and love through faith in Jesus Christ. Salvation can be found in no other name.

Historical Snapshot

Glossary: circumcision, grace, law, salvation

The Old Testament tells of how God created a good world, but evil and suffering entered. To bring the entire world back to himself, God called the Israelites, also called the Jews. He gave them laws to guide them in how to live righteously – that is, in a right way with God and others. It was through these people that God sent his Son, Jesus, who was born a Jew. Thus, the early followers of Jesus came from Israel, especially Jerusalem. Yet, the book of Acts shows how churches began springing up all over the ancient Roman Empire.

The early church faced the question of how Jewish and non-Jewish (Gentiles) followers of Jesus could worship together. Many churches in the Roman Empire were a mix of both Jewish and non-Jewish followers of Jesus. Since the origin of the church was Jewish, did the Gentiles need to follow Jewish customs too?

Jewish customs were based on the law that God had given to Israel. There were hundreds of laws governing every area of life. Circumcision especially was a sign that someone was in a relationship with God. Some Jewish followers of Jesus, called Judaizers, insisted that a few of these regulations, especially the practice of circumcision, were necessary for salvation. Simple faith in Jesus alone was not enough, they taught. Even non-Jews should follow these laws to be right with God. In his letter to the Galatian churches, Paul responds to these Judaizers' influence. Acts 15 shares another crucial event where the church leaders gathered to discuss this. They were clear: salvation is by grace alone.

However, this is not just a concern of the first-century. Throughout history and today, there have been other efforts to add something to our salvation. The message of Galatians is very relevant today.

Additional Note to the Leader: Perhaps your group might wonder, What is our relationship to the law? So do we have to keep the 10 Commandments? Are they different from laws such as circumcision and sacrifice? What about laws like those found in Leviticus 19:19, "Do not wear clothing woven of two kinds of material"? Questions like these may come up as early as lesson 2. You may want to encourage group members to keep thinking about a believer's relationship to the law and save their questions for lesson 4, as Paul will share the purpose of the law. Yet, it is important to honor the group as well. If they do ask questions about this, use questions to help them explore. Here is a quick overview to support you and your group. In typical DYB fashion, let's use questions:

- Where does the law fall within the whole of God's story?
  The Old Testament law was given as part of the covenant with Israel (Exodus 19). It gave laws to govern a nation, and revealed guidelines for righteous behavior and how to live with a righteous God.
- How does Jesus treat the law? He obeys it, teaches it, and fulfills it (Matthew 5:17; Luke 22:20; Hebrews 8:6, 13).
- What does the New Testament say about the Old Testament law? Paul's teaching in Galatians is important: that the law points us to Christ. It shows the standards for righteous behavior, which we fail. So it shows us our need (Galatians 4:24-25). Paul also emphasizes Christ's fulfillment (Galatians 4:6-7). In other letters, Paul reminds us that we can still learn from the law as it still shows principles for righteous living (Romans 15:4; 2 Timothy 3:16-17). Jesus affirms its essence (Matthew 5-7; 22:34-40).
- So if the New Testament says we are still to learn from the law, how do we learn from it? We still obey the principles of law (as filtered through the perfect life and death of Jesus) out of love for God. The Discover Your Bible approach is helpful to rightly learn from the law: *observation* in the biblical and historical context (understanding what it meant to the original audience); *interpretation* (understanding differences between the original audience and us; looking for the principle; filtering it through Jesus and the New Testament); and *application* (situating the principle in light of Jesus and our lives). We can understand then that some parts of the law are historically situated and completely fulfilled in Christ (circumcision and sacrifices). The principles there point us to Christ. We can understand that other parts, such as the Ten Commandments, still serve as guides to right living. But we do this not to be saved, but because we are filled with the life of Christ who authored the laws, and obeyed the laws perfectly.
- How does the law point us to the gospel? In summary, the law shows us a holy God and his right and wise ways for living in light of his presence; we still learn about his character through the principles. The law shows us our need, how we fall short and fail to keep it.

The law shows us Jesus, who perfectly kept it, yet took on the curse of the law for us. Then the principles of the law rightly interpreted serve as one facet of the biblical guide to understand the character of God, and how to live before him in the power of the Spirit in the new covenant.

For further reading, see: J. Daniel Hay's article on "Applying the Old Testament Law Today" from *Bibliotheca Sacra* 158: 629 (2001): 21-35, or the chapter in Gordon D. Fee and Douglas Stuart's *How to Read the Bible for All Its Worth*.

GOD'S STORY

CREATION
- God Creates: Creation

FALL
- The Fall

REDEMPTION
- God Promises a Rescuer: Adam & Eve
- God Promises to Preserve Creation: Noah
- God Promises a Blessing to All Peoples: Abraham
- God Promises to Lead His People: Moses, the Exodus, and the Law
- God Promises an Eternal King: David, Kings of Israel & Judah
- God Judges: The Exile
- God Remains Faithful: Return, Diaspora, & Waiting

GALATIANS

- **GOD RESCUES: JESUS** — Birth, Ministry, Death, Resurrection, & Ascension
- God Sends the Holy Spirit: Pentecost
- God Sends the Church: Acts & the Letters

NEW CREATION
- God Restores All Things: New Creation

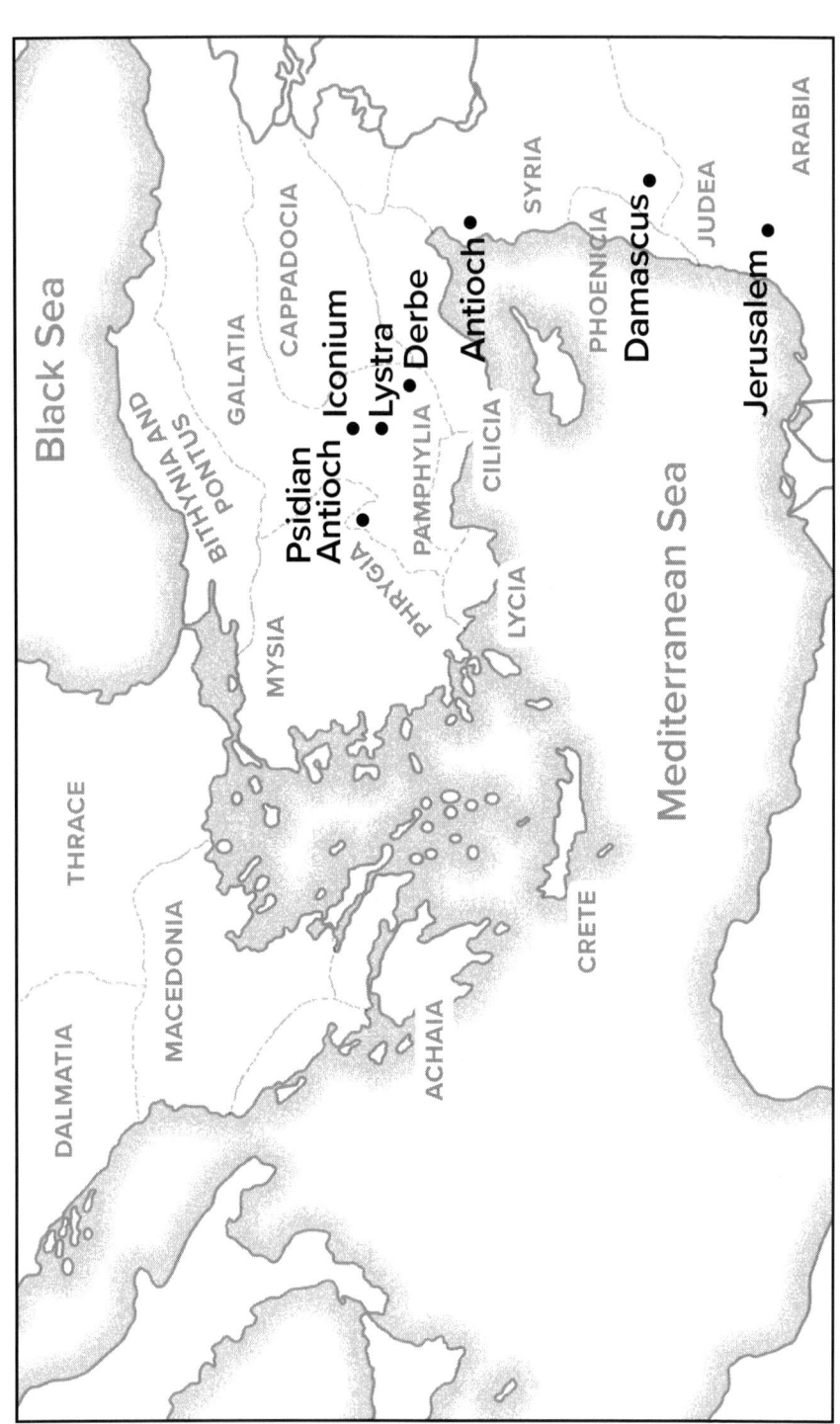

Glossary of Terms

Abba: An intimate term meaning "Father" in Aramaic, the common language of Jesus' day in Judea (Mark 14:36; Romans 8:15; Galatians 4:6).

Abraham (Abram): The father of the Jewish people. The Jews attached great importance in being the biological descendants of Abraham who would receive his blessing (Genesis 12:1-3). Abraham is also called the father of all believers (Romans 4:9-12, 20-25; 9:7-8). He was the first to receive the sign of circumcision, and an example of faith (Genesis 17; 11:26-25:10).

Amen: Often used at the conclusion of a prayer to express agreement and approval (Galatians 1:5; 6:18; Romans 11:33-36; Ephesians 3:14-21).

Angel: A messenger of God who carries out his will in this world and serves those who belong to God (Daniel 6:22; Luke 1:19; Hebrews 1:14).

Apostle: Meaning "one sent forth." The apostles were leaders in the early Christian church. They were chosen from those who had seen the Lord Jesus and who had witnessed his resurrection (1 Corinthians 9:1-2).

Baptize: To immerse in or wash with water. This act identifies a new believer with Christ and symbolizes the washing away of sin through Christ's sacrifice on the cross (Matthew 3:13-17; Acts 2:38-39).

Barnabas: A Jewish Christian who accompanied Paul in his missionary work (Acts 13:1-3). He was called "son of encouragement" in Acts 4:36. In Acts 9, Barnabas speaks on Paul's behalf, after his conversion, to Christians who are distrustful of Paul.

Blessing: Favor and kindness. In both the Old and New Testaments, blessing is relational, as one is in right relationship with God (Numbers 6:24-27). In the Old Testament, the material blessings are an outward sign of the relational blessing. In the New Testament, the emphasis of blessing is from our adoption into God's family (Galatians 3:7-9; Ephesians 1:3-5). It is clear that a person can be blessed and suffer at the same time (Matthew 5:3-11; James 1:12; 1 Peter 3:14, 4:14).

Book of the Law: The first five books of the Bible, which contain the law given to the Israelites and the narrative behind it. See "law."

Brother and sister: One who believes in Jesus Christ; a Christian.

Burden: Refers to any struggle or need. In Galatians 6:2, the word is the Greek *baros*, a heavy load. In 6:5, "load" is the Greek *phortion*, a smaller traveling pack.

Circumcision: Removal of the male foreskin that signified entrance into the Jewish faith. For the Jews it was an outward sign of

God's covenant with Abraham (Genesis 11:9-14) and symbolized cutting away sin from one's life. It was a mark of keeping the law. True circumcision is of the heart, not of the flesh (Romans 2:25; 3:30).

Covenant: A mutually binding agreement between two parties. God made covenants with his chosen people, Israel (most notably with Noah, Abraham, Israel through Moses, and David; Genesis 9:9-17; 15; Exodus 19; 2 Samuel 7).

Cross of Christ: Refers to Christ's suffering and death on the cross at Golgotha. This was referred to as crucifixion. It was an extremely painful, shameful death reserved for the worst criminals. Particularly for the Jews, not only was it shameful, it was considered cursed and unclean (Deuteronomy 21:23; Galatians 3:13).

Curse: God's sentence of punishment on those who disobey the law (Deuteronomy 11:26-28).

Debauchery: Open and shameless indulgence in sensual pleasures.

Elemental spiritual forces of the world: This could refer to the rules or forces of other religions, or the entire old order creation. These are "of the world" in the sense that they do not come from the new life of faith in Christ, the "new creation" (Galatians 6:15; 2 Corinthians 5:17). Paul mentions these in Galatians 4:6, 9; and Colossians 2:8, 20.

Eternal life: The state of being forgiven and loved by God. This life begins when one receives Jesus Christ by faith as Savior and Lord. Having eternal life does not mean believers will never die, but that they will enjoy eternal fellowship with God – both in this life and after death (John 3:16, 36; 17:3; Romans 6:23).

Faith: "Being sure of what we hope for and certain of what we do not see" (Hebrews 11:1). True saving faith consists of knowledge and confidence: a sure knowledge by which one accepts as true all that God has revealed in the Bible, and a confidence that all one's sins are forgiven for Christ's sake.

Family of believers: All who believe in Jesus Christ as Savior. Every Christian is a child of God and a brother or sister to other believers (John 1:12).

Flesh: In Galatians, Paul uses this term to refer to human efforts apart from God; the sinful state of human beings (Ephesians 2:3; Colossians 2:11-13).

Galatia: A province in the central region of Asia Minor, visited by Paul during his missionary journeys (perhaps Acts 13-14).

Gentiles: All people who are not Jews; this would include Greeks and the Galatians (Acts 10-11; Romans 16:25-27).

Glory: Splendor, majesty, power, worth, excellence of quality and character. In the Old Testament God's glory was often represented in a cloud (Exodus 33:12-34:7; also Exodus 14:14; Isaiah 6:3; Revelation 4:11).

Grace: God's kindness, unmerited favor, and forgiving love (John 1:17; Ephesians 2:6-10).

Gospel: Literally means "good news." The gospel is the message that God's Son, Jesus Christ, took the punishment for our sins upon himself, dying on the cross and rising again for the salvation of his people; that he ascended into heaven; and that he will some day return to establish his kingdom (1 Corinthians 15:1-4).

Hagar: The Egyptian handmaid of Sarah, Abraham's wife. Because Sarah was barren, she gave Hagar to Abraham in an attempt to produce an heir, in spite of God's promise that Sarah herself would bear a child. In Galatians, Paul uses Hagar as a metaphor for those Jewish believers who try to achieve salvation through their own efforts, not through faith in God's promise (Genesis 16; 21).

Holy Spirit: The third "person" of God (with Jesus and God the Father; together, the three persons are one being. This is called the Trinity). The Spirit of God comes to live in God's people to guarantee that they will receive all of God's promises and to empower them to live holy lives. For more of the Spirit's work, see Acts 1:8; Romans 8:1-2, 10-11; 1 Thessalonians 1:5; 2 Peter 1:21.

Hypocrisy: Pretending to be virtuous or religious without really being so. It is derived from the Greek word for actor (Matthew 6:1-18).

Idolatry: The worship of a physical object, a spirit, or an idea as a god. An idol can be anything more important to a person than God, something they look to for satisfaction or blessing or fulfillment, and that occupies their heart and mind and energy more than God (Psalm 115:3-8; 1 Corinthians 8:4-6; 10:14).

Israel: The people whom God formed a covenant with to be his representatives. It was originally the name given by God to the patriarch Jacob (Genesis 32:28), who had twelve sons who became the nation of Israel.

Impurity: Having one's life soiled with sins (those acts of disobedience that separate us from God) (Ephesians 5:3; Colossians 3:5).

Isaac: Son of Sarah and Abraham, born by God's promise when Sarah was well past child-bearing age (Genesis 15; 21).

Ishmael: Son of Hagar and Abraham (Genesis 16; 21).

James: A leader in the early church and head of the church in Jerusalem. This James is generally regarded as a brother of Jesus (Acts 15:13; Galatians 1:19; 2:9).

Jerusalem: Israel's capital city, central to the Jewish religion and its laws. Jerusalem also became the place where the Christian faith began.

Jesus Christ: The sinless Son of God, who gave his life as a payment for sin. Jesus was a common name, meaning "Savior." Christ is a title meaning "Anointed One," that was used in the Old Testament for a promised savior. Jesus is true God, along with the Father and the Holy Spirit (Matthew 1:21; 16:16).

John: One of the original twelve apostles and a leader in the Jerusalem church (Matthew 4:18-21).

Judaizers: Jewish Christians who believed that the ceremonial laws of the Old Testament were still required for salvation.

Justification (justify, justified): God's declaration that believers are pardoned of sin because of Jesus' sacrifice on the cross. If I believe in Christ, God looks at me "just-as-if-I'd" never sinned (Isaiah 53:10-11; Romans 3:21-31).

Kingdom of God: God's rule over his creation, especially over his people's lives (Mark 1:14-15; Romans 14:17; Colossians 1:13-14).

Know: In Galatians 4:9, "to know" connotes an intimate, personal "knowing" (Galatians 4:6-7; John 14:7, 17; 17:23).

Law: (1) The Ten Commandments and the hundreds of ceremonial laws given to the nation of Israel by God and recorded in the Old Testament. Jews understood this was the way to live righteously. Circumcision was a symbol of keeping the law. The demands of the law were fulfilled when Jesus Christ offered himself as a perfect sacrifice for sins on the cross (Matthew 22:37-39). (2) The law could also be used to refer to the first five books of the Bible (Genesis, Exodus, Leviticus, Numbers, Deuteronomy) which contained the laws and stories of the formation of God's people (e.g., Abraham, Sarah, Hagar, Isaac, etc.).

Mediator: One who intervenes between two parties to reconcile them. Jesus Christ is the only mediator between God and humankind (1 Timothy 2:5; Hebrews 8:6; 9:15).

Mercy: God's free and undeserved compassion. To be more precise, it refers to showing leniency by holding back punishment even if justice calls for it (see Micah 7:18-19).

Miracle: An act performed by supernatural power. The Gospels and Acts recount how God often confirmed his message of salvation in Christ with miracles (Mark 6:1-3; Acts 2:22; 14:3).

Mount Sinai: The mountain in the Desert of Sinai on which Moses received the Ten Commandments from God (Exodus 19).

New creation: A cleansed and restored relationship with God, in which all the sins of the past are forgiven, wiped clean. Through the Spirit the believer receives the power to live a new and holy life (2 Corinthians 5:17).

Orgies: Drunken revelry; excessive sexual indulgence.

Paul: A Jew born in Tarsus; he is also called Saul. Before his conversion to Christ, Paul actively persecuted the early church. After his conversion Paul became an apostle and one of the most important missionaries to the Gentiles (Acts 9).

Peace: Peace, or *shalom*, is an ancient Hebrew word that denotes total well-being, not merely an absence of strife but a fullness of life and harmony (John 14:27; Acts 10:36; Colossians 3:15).

Peter (Cephas): One of the original twelve apostles, also known as Simon. Peter was a prominent and fearless preacher of the gospel. Cephas is Peter's Aramaic name; Aramaic was a common language where Peter lived (Matthew 4:18-21).

Redeem (redemption): To buy something back with a ransom payment; refers here to God's paying the penalty of sin by Christ's death on the cross and thereby winning back sinners who would otherwise have died under the law's punishment (Mark 10:45.)

Revelation: God's communicating or revealing divine truth to humans (Ephesians 1:17; 3:3).

Righteous (righteousness): Free from guilt or sin. God regards us as righteous through Christ when we are joined to him by faith (Romans 3:20-22; 2 Corinthians 5:21).

Salvation: Eternal deliverance from the power and penalty of sin; salvation is possible only through the finished work of Jesus Christ, in whom we believe as Savior and Lord (John 3:16; 14:6). Jesus' work also leads to the salvation and restoration of God's creation, which is now in "bondage to decay" (Romans 8:21).

Sarah: Abraham's wife and an important woman in Israel's history. She was childless for many years, until God miraculously gave her a promised son when she was 90 or 91 years old (Genesis 11:29-30; 18:9-14).

Seed: Human descendants.

Sexual immorality: Illegitimate sexual relations; marital unfaithfulness.

Sin: Disobedience to God's will (as he reveals it in human conscience and in his Word, the Bible) (Romans 6:23; James 4:17).

Sons: Paul uses "sons" to refer to all of God's children, both male and female. Because in the ancient world, sons were recognized as heirs, Paul uses the masculine to refer to the full rights that all – men and women – have in Christ.

Titus: A Christian of Gentile background who worked with Paul and had never been circumcised (2 Corinthians 8:23; Titus 1:4).

Transgression: See **sin.**

Yeast: Symbolizes evil or false teaching that can spread through believers like yeast through dough (Mark 8:15; 1 Corinthians 15:6-7).

Yoke: Wooden bar shaped to fit over a person's shoulders to enable him or her to carry a heavy load (Matthew 11:28-29).

Zealous: Full of eagerness and ardent interest (Romans 12:11).

1 Galatians 1:1-24
A Different Gospel

Optional Share Question

What do you like most about change?

Optional share questions introduce a simple idea for a "warm-up" to help everyone get acquainted and to help put newcomers at ease. You may choose to adapt them to your group. The following are characteristics of good warm-up questions: personal to your group; can be briefly answered; connect to the lesson; and something everyone, including newcomers, can answer; light-hearted and non-threatening.

This share question helps lead into the following lesson, where there is negative change (the Galatians deserting the gospel) and positive change (in Paul's life).

Getting Started

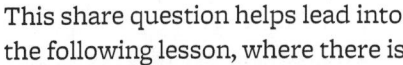

Glossary: apostle, faith, gospel, Jesus Christ, Paul, salvation

Like a malignant tumor, a dangerous and false teaching is growing among the Galatian churches. Stakes are high. It threatens to destroy. In this chapter, we will see how Paul quickly and fervently responds to this danger. We will be invited to let our hearts be encouraged, protected, and zealous as well.

As you begin to study this letter, engage yourself in the debate that is about to unfold. Ask yourself, *Who is involved in this debate? What is the controversy? Why is it important? Why is it important to us today?*

The introduction will greatly help in understanding Paul's opening arguments. This briefly explains the false teaching in the Galatian churches. Also note the glossary of terms included in this study, which gives the meanings of difficult or unfamiliar terms you may find in your study.

Additional Note to the Leader: Many additional questions (with bullets and in italics) are included. These are only suggestions. They show a pattern, and help prompt for some of the crucial points. Do not feel you have to ask all of the questions. Use which ones are helpful for your group. Put them in your own words. Tailor the conversation to your group with one ear on the Holy Spirit, and the other on the group.

Discovering Together

1. Galatians 1:1-5

Glossary: apostle, Galatia, glory, grace, Jesus Christ, peace, redeem, sin

a. Who is the writer of this letter? To whom is it addressed?

Help all feel welcome by exploring the characters involved. The introduction will provide all the information needed. Paul is one of the apostles who leads the young Christian church, and has preached the gospel to most of the churches in the area known as Galatia.

The letter is addressed to a region of church. This letter is generally assumed to have been written soon after one of Paul's visits to those churches to be read and passed from church to church.

b. Why is Paul qualified to write this letter?

- *Who called Paul to be an apostle?*
- *What does this say about God's concern for the people in the remote regions of the Roman Empire?*
- *How does Paul's call show his authority?*
- *Who else sends their greetings to the church in Galatia? (v. 2)*

As the founder, Paul knows the church; he has authority in the church. More importantly, he is sent from God the Father and Jesus himself. God cared about these remote regions of the Roman Empire. God himself sends his witness there.

Paul mentions the support of the other workers in the gospel who accompany him on his travels – "and all the brothers with me" (v. 2). This also adds to his support and authority. They are in agreement with him.

c. How does the author greet his readers?

- *What is the source of this grace and peace?*
- *Think back to the situation in the Galatian church from the "Historical Snapshot." Why would these words be an especially meaningful greeting to the early church?*
- *How are grace and peace related to each other? To our relationship with God?*

Paul greets the churches in Galatia with these words: "Grace and peace." These were common greetings in the Greek and Hebrew cultures. But Paul adds the rich Christian meaning; these are in the glossary.

The Galatian churches are troubled with false teaching from within and persecution from without. Paul's greeting brings a sense of godly favor to these confused believers. God himself is still extending grace and peace.

Groups more familiar with the Bible may also want to discuss how grace and peace describe the essence of the Christian life. In his commentary on Galatians, Martin Luther, the sixteenth-century German Reformer, makes the point that "grace contains the remission of sins; peace a quiet and joyful conscience.... Therefore, Paul, in all the greetings of his epistles, sets grace and peace against sin and an evil conscience." God's grace leads to peace with God, others, and self.

d. What do you learn about God, Jesus, and you?

- *How is God described? What does he desire? Why? What is our relationship with God through Jesus?*
- *What does it mean that Christ "gave himself" (see Matthew 20:28; Romans 4:25; Galatians 2:20)?*
- *What did that accomplish, according to verse 4?*
- *What does "this present evil age" refer to? Why might Paul describe it this way?*
- *Why do we need rescuing?*
- *How do verses 3-5 give the gospel? What is the gospel in your own words?*

Paul begins with a snapshot of the gospel: God willed that Jesus would redeem us from our sins (including legalism).

Remember that one way to promote the evangelistic purpose of this Bible study is to highlight specific references to God. Use these to introduce your group members to the One who reveals himself in his Word. Paul often refers to God in very descriptive terms. These references are rich with information on who God is, what he has done, and what he is able to do in and through his Spirit and people.

So what do we see about God? God is our Father, and he willed that Jesus would save us. We are loved by God! Jesus is Lord, a Lord who gave himself. "This present evil age" refers to the world system that is still under sin (Ephesians 1:21). We will discover more about the ways of "this present evil age" in the verses and chapters that follow. Redemption results in glory to God.

Paul presents the gospel: Christ's sacrifice on the cross is all that is needed for salvation. Believers do not have to supplement their faith in Christ with good works or ceremonial regulations in order to receive salvation. That theme may not be obvious to your group yet, but through questions you can open the door to their beginning realization. The gospel is a thing of beauty – it can be stated in a few sentences, yet takes a lifetime to discover.

2. Galatians 1:6-9

Glossary: angel, curse, gospel

a. What is the trouble in the churches of Galatia?

- *What tone of voice do you detect in Paul's words?*
- *How does this differ from Philippians 1:1-6?*
- *Why do you think Paul feels so strongly for the Galatian Christians?*
- *If you were a member of the Galatian church, how do you think you would feel receiving these words?*
- *How might Paul's concern show God's concern as well?*

The trouble is that they are turning to a different gospel. It is apparent that in this letter Paul feels the seriousness of the subject very deeply. If desired, you could read Philippians 1:1-6 and compare it to the greeting here. Paul usually begins his letters with at least a few words of praise for his readers, but here he omits any praise in his sense of urgency.

Frustration, concern, disbelief at the churches' ability to leave the truth so quickly – all these may be part of Paul's feelings as he writes these words. It must hurt Paul that he is separated by distance from his friends and has to deal with this crucial issue in a letter rather than face to face. Help your group see that Paul loves these young Christians very much. He is, in a sense, their spiritual father and they his children (Galatians 4:19).

b. How does Paul describe the "different gospel" and what others are trying to do?

- *Is there another gospel? If so, is the different gospel a gospel at all? Does this seem to touch the heart of the gospel, or be an unimportant matter?*
- *If there is only one gospel, what do we learn about salvation? Is there salvation in another gospel?*
- *What do we learn about the true gospel?*
- *How does the teaching there is one gospel relate to some teaching we hear today?*

"Different," "a desertion," "no gospel at all," "confusion" "perversion" "other" are ways that Paul describes this different gospel. Those who preach a different gospel are under God's curse. On the flipside, the true gospel is held up as the way to God. The gift of grace is the realm we live in now.

Paul's vehement anger against those who are "trying to pervert the gospel of Christ" may take some group members aback. Do not go too deeply into the Galatian heresy at this point; let your group members discover it as they work through the coming lessons. But do help group members discover that the very core of the gospel is at stake here, and that is why Paul's anger is justifiably aroused. There is only one gospel, and one way to salvation.

The truth of one gospel is often denied in today's world, where many say that all religions lead to truth, or where churches or church leaders add to the gospel, saying that our actions are needed for salvation. This may or may not be something you would like to discuss with your group. Be sensitive to the group and to the Holy Spirit.

To explore Paul's words against the false teachers:

- *Why does he condemn the false teachers so strongly?*

- *How does he feel about those who preach a false gospel?*
- *What does it mean to be under God's curse? How do they remove themselves from God's grace by denying the true gospel?*

Paul's judgment is strong; those who preach a gospel other than that of Jesus Christ risk the possibility of God's eternal judgment. There can be no worse fate. Again, this reveals the extreme gravity of the situation in the Galatian churches. They remove themselves from God's truth, and there is no other way and no other gospel. They have cut themselves off from life, and are leading others to do the same.

Do not let this conversation become focused on judging others who might have different perspectives but still fall within orthodox Christianity.

Ephesians 2:8-10, also written by Paul, might be a helpful summary. We are saved by grace through faith, not by works. Works will overflow from a new heart given by grace.

3. Galatians 1:10
What is Paul's ultimate motivation in making these charges?

- *As the "Getting Started" said, this is a debate. What might others accuse Paul of that he is responding to in verse 10?*
- *How might Paul's audience feel after reading verses 6-9? Might it sound to them as though Paul is softening his words to win their approval or to please them? What does this say about his motivation?*
- *To whom alone does Paul hold himself accountable? How can Paul have the confidence to please God alone? How can we?*
- *Is it possible to try to please God and others at the same time? How is this like trying to serve two masters? (See Matthew 6:24.)*

Paul's motivation is to serve God. Apparently Paul's critics have charged him with trying to win the favor of people, presenting a gospel that he feels will appeal to his hearers. Certainly not needing to be circumcised is more appealing to the Gentiles! However, Paul's stinging criticism against any person – be it angel, apostle, or anyone else – who teaches a false gospel quickly proves this accusation false.

His first concern, then and always, is the gospel of Christ. His loyalty is to God, not to people (which frees him to love, as we will see). He calls himself a servant, or slave, of Christ. In Paul's day a slave could have only one master. The word *still* implies that Paul has at one time lived to gain others' admiration and approval. The passage that follows deals with the dramatic change in Paul's life that brought him into God's service.

4. Galatians 1:11-17

Glossary: revelation

a. Who is the source of the gospel Paul preached?

- *How does it impact you that the gospel is from God himself? (1 Thessalonians 2:13)*
- *What does the source say about the power of the gospel?*
- *What does this say about the credibility of what we read? How does this shape the trust you put in the gospel and God's Word?*

The gospel is God's revelation. Verses 11 and 12 are vital to understanding Paul's defense, particularly as he recounts his conversion and prior ministry through chapter 2. There is no question that Paul's concern is for the gospel. That is why he takes pains to remind the Galatian Christians of what they undoubtedly know already: this gospel came to Paul by revelation of Jesus Christ (see Ephesians 3:2-6).

Paul not only states where the gospel is from, but also what does not influence him:

- *What does Paul say does not influence him?*
- *What accusations may Paul be responding to here?*
- *What authority does this lend to Paul's words?*

Paul is not, in other words, passing along his own teaching nor is he simply retelling the teachings of another person. Others may accuse him of coming up with his own teaching, but he says his gospel is directly from God.

b. What change happened in Paul's life and how? What makes it seem unlikely that Paul would ever have changed?

- *Why does he mention this? How does it add credibility to his argument?*
- *Who changed him?*

- *What was Paul noted for prior to his conversion to Christianity?*
- *How do our testimonies also show the power of the gospel?*

He had persecuted those who believed in the gospel; now he serves the church. Paul clearly emphasizes the dramatic turnaround in his life at the point of his conversion. God changed him. His conversion shows the power and authenticity of his gospel, and the authenticity of the call of God. He is not creating his own gospel, but only carrying out God's call and sharing God's truth. If there is time, sharing a brief testimony or two can help newcomers see how God continues to work. For more background information on Paul's former life and dramatic conversion, read Acts 8 and 9.

If your conversation turns toward God's call of Paul, you may use follow up questions similar to these:

- *When did God know Paul? What does that say about God?*
- *How is God's call described in verse 15? Why is it grace?*
- *What did God reveal to Paul?*
- *How is it life-changing to see Jesus?*
- *What was Paul's immediate response to God's calling?*
- *Why is it significant that Paul was not taught under the authority of the established church?*
- *Whom does Paul claim as his sole and absolute authority?*
- *How does Paul's account establish his claim to his qualifications to preach the true gospel? How does God's call here show God's power and control in a person's life? What comfort does this offer a believer?*

Like Jeremiah (Jeremiah 1:5), God knew Paul and knew his call on his life before he was born. Paul did nothing to earn God's grace – in fact, his trying to destroy the church was every reason not to call Paul! But this is the power of God. Seeing Jesus, seeing who God truly is in the Son and through the Son, is life changing.

Paul did not consult others; rather, he went to Arabia immediately. This was likely for a time of study, to search the Scriptures. Paul will show how his gospel is the same as what the other apostles are teaching; but here he is clearly showing that his gospel is divine. God is the sole authority, and has clearly called Paul.

5. Galatians 1:18-20

Glossary: Peter (Cephas), James

a. What contact did Paul have with the other apostles after receiving his calling from God?

- *How does this affirm Paul's point?*
- *Put yourself in the Galatian's shoes, with two different teachers claiming authority. Why might it be important to mention the other apostles? What authority do they have?*

Paul saw Peter (Cephas) and James three years after God's call. He reaffirms his point that he did not learn the gospel from other believers.

The apostles of the early church are a group of leaders whose authority is recognized because (1) they have been personally taught by Jesus and (2) they are eyewitnesses to his resurrection.

b. Why do you suppose Paul emphasizes this point to his readers?

- *If you were in Galatia, and heard two different "gospels," what might you be wondering? How might this section help you know whom to trust?*
- *What tells us that this is a very important point for Paul to make? (See v. 20.)*
- *How do we also face the dilemma of whom to trust? What criteria do we look for?*

Paul appeals to the witness of God that he is telling the Galatians the truth in this matter. The Galatians must be confused (v. 7), and wonder whom to trust. Paul is giving point after point of why they can trust him.

6. Galatians 1:21-24

a. What have the churches in Judea heard about Paul?

b. How have they responded to Paul's ministry?

- *How might you respond if someone who formerly persecuted you or people you know came to visit your church?*

- *How does the Judean Christians' faith in his ministry confirm Paul's calling as a true messenger from God?*

Paul has lived most of his life in the province of Judea and has persecuted many of the Christian churches in that region (Acts 8:13; 9:10). The Judean Christians know his history – and yet they accept him. The reaction of the Judean believers indicates that Paul's conversion is genuine and that the gospel he preaches is fully trustworthy.

As you follow Paul's brief biography, you may want to use a map to find the places he mentions. Do not, however, focus on the history of Paul's life so much as on the point he is trying to establish: he owes his gospel to God's revelation, not to human teaching.

To summarize, you may consider asking the following questions:

- *According to what you have read so far, what would you say is Paul's purpose in writing this letter?*
- *What have we learned about the gospel so far? What is the content? How many are there? Who gives the gospel?*
- *What is Paul's main point in verses 11-24?*

Although you have not yet studied in depth the heresy plaguing the Galatian churches, your group should know the basic issues at stake: (1) there is one gospel which calls us to "live in the grace of Christ" (v. 6) and (2) the gospel Paul preaches is God's revelation, not human instruction.

As you conclude, be sensitive to the possibility that the force of Paul's emotion in the opening sections may bewilder some members. Let their emotions provoke curiosity and questions. Ask about these, listen, and let it create hunger to learn more. Help them hold onto this hunger for the coming weeks as you more fully discover the letter to the Galatians together.

Discovering Our Stories

a. What attitude are we to have toward the gospel?

- *How do we seek the true gospel in today's world?*

b. What does pleasing God first look like in daily life?

- *How might pleasing God sometimes mean displeasing people?*

c. God used Paul's story to further the gospel message. How might God use your/our stories to further the gospel message?

d. What is your next step as a result of this study?

e. Read Psalm 119:9-24; Paul surely shared the attitude of the psalmist. Make it your prayer as well.

With question d, encourage your group members to specify one thing that they will really take to heart this week. We learn by doing; our knowledge needs to be specifically brought into our lives. Head, heart, or hands may provide a useful perspective. What might they believe differently? Feel as a result of this? Do as a result?

Keep the safety of the group in mind as you discuss application. While change happens in specifics, group members may not yet be comfortable sharing personal specifics. Or perhaps sharing in pairs might feel safer for your group members. Also, this can provide specific ways to pray for each other, and hold each other accountable in the following week if your group desires.

More to Discover

The following verses will help you understand more about what is contained in the parentheses. Each will help deepen understanding and discussion.

Question 1d | Matthew 20:28; Romans 4:25; Galatians 2:20 (Christ "gave himself")

Ephesians 1:21 (this present evil age)

2a | Philippians 1:1-6 (a typical greeting from Paul)

Galatians 4:19 (Paul's attitude toward the Galatians)

2b | 1 Corinthians 15:1-5; Ephesians 2:8-10 (the gospel)

3 | Matthew 6:24 (pleasing God and others)

4a | Ephesians 3:2-6; 1 Thessalonians 2:13 (source of the gospel)

4b | Jeremiah 1:5 ("set me apart")

Acts 7:58-8:3; 9:1-30 (Paul's transformation)

6b | Acts 8:13; 9:10 (how Paul persecuted the churches)

The verses in the "More to Discover" all come from the additional notes in the leader guide, so that each member is able to access these. If you choose to use one of the verses in the Leader Guide, you may help your group realize they too have those listed in the "More to Discover".

2 Galatians 2:1-21
Defending the Faith

Optional Share Question

Name one of the most influential people in your life.

Model keeping answers brief. In this lesson we'll meet a number of influential people – for better or for worse.

Getting Started

Chapter 1 records Paul's passionate defense of the authenticity of the gospel he preaches. He makes it very clear to his readers that the gospel he preaches is not of human origin but from God. Here he continues to set his teaching in the context of the wider church. We get a unique glimpse into the interactions of the early church, the boldness that comes from the gospel, and what it means to live in light of that.

Additional Note to the Leader: As you prepare to lead this lesson, ask the Holy Spirit's guidance to help members understand both the historical issues behind Paul's teaching and the practical message it brings to us today. Pray for group members as we wrestle with questions such as, Are we saved by believing or by achieving? Does our faith depend solely in Christ's sacrifice, or do good works figure in as well?

You may sense that some members are struggling with some of the concepts or verses in today's lesson. Be sure to offer them extra time, if possible, to help clarify difficult terms or answer questions. Remember that many of the words that have so much meaning for Christians – grace, justification, sin, law, righteousness – may be unfamiliar to a newcomer. Pray that the Holy Spirit will make you sensitive to questions that some do not quite dare to ask. Pray that the message of salvation through faith in Christ will shine clearly through the Scriptures.

If questions come up about the relationship of believers today to the law, the additional note to the leader following the "Historical Snapshot" may provide support. However, you may encourage the group to save their questions for lesson 4, when Paul talks about the purpose of the law more clearly.

Discovering Together

1. **Galatians 2:1-5**

   Glossary: apostle, Barnabas, circumcision, Gentiles, gospel, Jerusalem, Judaizers, Titus

   a. What reasons prompted Paul to go to Jerusalem? Why might he have brought Titus?

   - *What were Paul's fears, and how did he deal with them?*
   - *What is the "race" that Paul was running? How might he have been running it "in vain"?*
   - *Why is it important that Paul mentions Titus is a Greek, that is, a Gentile?*
   - *Why might Titus be compelled to be circumcised? If he was, how would that reflect on Paul's gospel and ministry?*

   God directed Paul by revelation to go to Jerusalem. Paul did so obediently, speaking to the apostles, probably in private, regarding his message and teaching. Paul, though convinced that the gospel he taught was the true one, was concerned that his work among the Gentiles not be at odds with the aims and message of the rest of the church. He wanted to confirm the leaders would support his ministry to the Gentiles.

   Paul feared he was running in vain. He did not think the gospel was in vain or untrue but he knew that the apostles' agreement with him would have an impact on his ministry. He was afraid that his ministry to the Gentiles would not be welcomed, and that demands would be placed on them that would undermine his proclamation of the gospel.

   Paul likely brought Titus because he was a trusted friend, but his status as a Gentile Christian who had not been circumcised may have also been helpful support. Judaizers would be forced to say whether they thought circumcision was necessary for Titus. For the Jews, circumcision was a sign of being in the people of God. Titus's presence gave Paul opportunity to defend what he believed to be the heart of the gospel he had preached among the Gentiles. The "Introduction," and glossary "Jerusalem" and "circumcision" should provide the needed background.

b. What are the people who oppose Paul seeking to do?

- *What freedom is Paul referring to (v. 4)? How does Titus's example illustrate freedom? What does Titus need in order to approach God?*
- *What kind of slavery do his opponents want to impose? How might this slavery be related to the issue of circumcision?*
- *Do you think Paul's opponents think they are promoting slavery? Why or why not? What do we learn from this?*
- *Are there things today that would be equivalent to circumcision and be a form of slavery? How can we be aware? What do we need in order to approach God? How might some try to add to this list?*

Paul's opponents try to attack the "freedom we have in Christ Jesus and to make us slaves" (v. 4). The freedom we have is freedom from having to obey the law in order to be accepted by God. We are free because we are accepted by God's grace through faith in Christ. We are free to live a life of love, service, holiness. We are free to be slaves to righteousness (Romans 6:18), not to do whatever we desire. Exploring Titus's situation as an example of freedom may help your group understand freedom. He is not required to do some external rite in order to be accepted by God, or live a righteous life. We will continue to discover more about freedom as we continue through this study. Some group members may bring in their own cultural idea of freedom; help them define freedom from the text.

Paul's opponents want to impose law keeping, particularly circumcision. Paul sees this as slavery. It seems that the Judaizers believe that faith in Christ is not enough for salvation. Since circumcision is a sign of acceptance in the people of God, they feel that the Gentiles need this sign also. Thus, because circumcision is such an important part of Jewish ceremonial law, it becomes a point around which many of the Judaizers rally. They insist that, as a symbol of obedience to the law, circumcision is also necessary as a sign of acceptance in the people of God.

Paul's opponents likely do not see it as slavery; they see it as a faithful way to honor God and necessary for salvation. We have to be aware, and discern carefully. Today, as well, things can be added on to the gospel: faith + our works, faith + tithing, faith + a certain sign of the Holy Spirit, etc. It is true that true faith will produce good works and fruit of the Holy Spirit, but these are not conditions for salvation.

c. What do we learn about the truth of the gospel? How does it affect us?

- *Why does Paul feel that this is such a vital point? What is at stake?*
- *How do Paul's strong feelings strike you? Why is this important to you?*
- *What kind of bondage will this false teaching put on the believers? On what will their salvation be based?*
- *How does this insistence on obedience to the law as a requirement for salvation attack the very heart of the gospel?*
- *How do we share this urgency? How might Paul grow his love of the gospel? How do we?*
- *How do you think God feels about the gospel?*

Paul is fighting for the truth of the gospel. Salvation is by God's grace. To believe otherwise is to undercut the true gospel and the unity of the faith in Jesus. The true gospel affects us because it is grounded in God's grace, and so gives us freedom in Christ, but it also reminds us of where our salvation lies and where it does not.

Some in your group may be learning about the gospel for the first time. Do not feel compelled to tell more than what is present in the text. Let them discover it as this letter unfolds the beauty of God's gospel. Help them see how important it was to Paul. His sense of urgency may impress them to consider why it is so important.

2. Galatians 2:6-10

Glossary: grace, James, John, Peter (Cephas)

a. How do these verses support Paul's argument so far? How did the leaders regard Paul's message? What did they recognize?

- *How does Paul regard the leaders of the church? What words does he use to describe them?*
- *Does their social standing make any difference in how he might preach the gospel?*
- *How does verse 9 identify these leaders?*
- *How did the leaders recognize God's validation of Paul's ministry?*
- *What did the leaders do to show their approval and acceptance?*
- *How can our congregations give the "right hand of fellowship" to other Christian groups in our communities? Why is it important to do so?*

Paul's purpose in meeting with the other apostles was to verify the authority of his ministry. The leaders added nothing to his message (v. 6), recognized God's commission of Paul (v. 7), and God's hand in his work (v. 8). They gave him the right hand of fellowship. In short, Paul's ministry was confirmed.

Paul does not regard the other apostles as authors of the gospel but as fellow servants. Verse 9 indicates that these leaders were James, Peter, and John. Paul's words do not show disrespect for the leaders, or hostility. Rather, he emphasizes that they were in full accord. They acknowledged he was proclaiming the full gospel. Thus, they agreed and added nothing to what Paul taught. He has both God's approval, and the other leaders' recognition.

It is likely that Paul presented his work to the leaders by giving evidence of the Holy Spirit's power behind his ministry: miracles, large numbers of converts, and a growing spiritual maturity in the Gentile churches (see also Galatians 3:5; 2 Corinthians 12:12). To show their acceptance, the leaders extended the right hand of fellowship – that is, they recognized Paul's gospel as truth and as their own.

b. Compare the ministries of Peter and Paul. How are they alike? How are they different?

- *Whom do they reach out to?*
- *Who commissions them?*
- *What message do they preach?*
- *Why is this important to include?*

As you discuss the ministries of Peter and Paul, your group should recognize that, other than the fact that they are aimed at different audiences (Jew versus Gentile), these ministries share much in common. The same God commissions them both. The same gospel is preached. Both show results by the Spirit.

This is important because, as Paul says in Galatians 1, there is only one gospel. Peter and Paul preach the same gospel. There is one gospel for Jews and Gentiles. There are no additional requirements that can exclude others.

c. What one request did the leaders make of Paul?

- *How does this request reflect God's concern? What do you learn about God?*

- *How are we to show this concern today in our faith community?*

God is concerned for the plight of the poor (see Psalm 125; Isaiah 25:4; 41:17; James 2:5). Jewish law contained many regulations protecting the needy and powerless. Remembering the poor was also an important part of the early church's ministry. James, one of the leaders Paul met with, wrote later to the churches, "Religion that God our Father accepts as pure and faultless is this: to look after orphans and widows in their distress . . ." (James 1:27).

3. Galatians 2:11-14
How did Peter change his behavior? Why was this change inconsistent with the gospel?

- *What ethnicity is Peter? What did Peter do before?*
- *What does eating show about fellowship and acceptance? What did his eating with Gentiles show about Peter's belief about how one becomes a full member of the family of God?*
- *What influenced Peter to change?*
- *How did Peter's actions deny his belief?*
- *What effect did this have on the believers with Peter?*
- *What do you learn about the truth of the gospel from these verses?*
- *How might our actions show the truth, or not show the truth, of the gospel to others?*

This is a second event, distinct from verses 1 to 10, which took place in Jerusalem. A simple question about location may help your group clarify this if necessary.

Peter was eating with Gentiles – this excluded them and rebuilt the distinction between Jew and Gentile. Peter's eating with Gentiles showed that they were fully part of the family of God, without following the law (Acts 10). He also believed one was right with God (justified) only by God's grace through faith in Christ. Faith in Christ – the message of Paul's gospel – was enough.

However, he changed when those from the circumcision group came. Peter acted in fear of humans (not the first time, Luke 22:54-62). Peter, a Jew, had freely accepted the Gentiles as one with him in the body of Christ. Now, he excluded them. If Peter knew that being circumcised was not necessary to be accepted by God, that Gentiles are fully welcomed by faith, he should keep eating with Gentiles and not draw other Christians away from the truth. He should keep showing that faith in Jesus is enough. His influence was great, and he led others astray. There were serious consequences to his failure in leadership.

If you have time, you could explore the confrontation as well.

- *What do we learn about the way Paul confronted Peter? How public was Peter's sin? How public was Paul's confrontation?*
- *What gave Paul boldness?*
- *What do we learn from this?*
- *Are there ways we face the temptation to ask others to behave like our church culture before we accept them?*

Peter's sin was public and had public ramifications, so Paul confronted him publicly. His sin excluded others, the opposite of Galatians 3:26-28. Peter was indicating that the Gentiles needed faith in Christ, plus to act like Jews, behave like Jews, in order to be accepted by him and by God.

Study Note: Eating in ancient Jewish culture was more than a social activity, but showed fellowship and acceptance. Jews were prohibited from eating with Gentiles (Acts 10:28). Jews highlighted the distinction between themselves as circumcised, law-keepers, and children of Abraham, and the uncircumcised, sinful Gentiles who did not have the law. Jesus lived out the true calling of Israel, to use their law as a light to all (Matthew 9:10-13; Acts 10:9-48; Micah 4:1-5; Deuteronomy 4:6-8).

4. Galatians 2:15-21

Glossary: crucifixion, justification, law, sin

a. Paul continues to address Peter. What does Paul say is the basis for being justified with God? How is one not justified? (v. 16)

- *How might Paul define justification? How might the Jews define justification? What is the difference? How would you define justification in your own words?*
- *What does it mean to have faith in Christ?*

- *How do the Jews view Gentiles in Ephesians 2:11? How do they use circumcision and their possession of the law to create division? How might they think of the Gentiles as sinners and themselves as righteous by the law?*
- *Does being Jewish by birth or following the law remove one from the category of sinner? What have Peter and Paul learned about how to be right with God?*

In verse 16 Paul makes the heart of the issue clear: all people are made right with God by faith in Jesus Christ (as Paul proclaims), not by works of the law (as the Jews might argue). In verse 15, Paul is not denying that Jews are sinners as well. He is referring to Jewish thought, which considers Gentiles sinful while Jews are right with God because of circumcision and the law (Ephesians 2:11). Peter and Paul have learned this distinction between Gentiles and Jews is demolished in Christ (Ephesians 2:11-14; Galatians 3:26-28).

Clarify your group's understanding of justification – and that it is available to all by faith, no matter their birth or history. Encourage your group to use the glossary, but take time to discuss this term.

As you discuss the very heart of the Christian gospel, be sure to allow the Holy Spirit to do the convicting in your group. Be sensitive to those who simply are not ready to accept this gospel, as well as to those who show evidence of spiritual awakening.

b. What are the Jews rebuilding? (See verses 12, 14, 16) What does rebuilding this result in, in verse 18? Why?

- *How might rebuilding the law undermine justification in Christ alone? If one is trying to rebuild the law, are they looking to their own acts or to Christ to be accepted by God? What is God's will for the way of salvation now? (John 14:6) How might trying to gain acceptance by the law be against God's will shown in Christ and be sin?*
- *How might rebuilding the law increase division between Jew and Gentile?*
- *What does Paul say God destroyed in Ephesians 2:11-14?*
- *What is the fulfillment of the law in Romans 13:10 and Galatians 5:14? How is the division created by the law not fulfilling the law of love?*
- *Are there examples of this lawbreaking today?*

- How does salvation by grace alone, in Christ alone, by faith alone mean that all who believe are welcomed, regardless of the way society views them?

Rebuilding the law made someone rely on their own works, instead of Jesus, for salvation. They are lawbreakers by denying the saving work of Christ. God's will is salvation through Christ. To try to be saved or live by another way is going against God's will the essence of sin. Equally important, adding to the law also meant rebuilding the division between Jew and Gentile. They are lawbreakers who add to the gospel and exclude people whom God saved by grace through faith. They fail to fulfill the law of love in Romans 13:10 and Galatians 5:14.

Peter and Paul find themselves among the sinners. First, they are among the sinners by acknowledging that they also need Christ for salvation and their own law-keeping is not enough. Second, they are among the "sinners" socially by being among the Gentiles (seen as "sinners" and outside the people of God by the Jews).

Do we abandon the law completely and live however we desire, including in sin? Faith in Christ, without works of the law, is sufficient not only for salvation, but also leads to living a new life according to the law of love – for God and for neighbor. True faith will lead to walking in the Spirit, with his fruit, and in love, which fulfills the law (Galatians 5:6, 14).

c. How does Paul describe his relationship with Christ?

- What image does Paul use to get across his point that leaving the old way of salvation behind is a "once for all" experience?
- What does it mean to "die to the law"?
- In what sense was he crucified with Christ?
- What takes the place of the law at the center of Paul's life? What now controls his desires, his plans, his work?
- What enables him to live a holy life?
- How does Paul describe Jesus in v. 20? What affect does this description have upon your relationship with Christ? How does Paul's very warm and personal description of Jesus in the last part of verse 20 contrast with the rigid demands of the law?
- Look at the personal pronouns, "me." How does it impress you that Christ died and gave himself for you personally?

- *How do you experience Christ's life in you?*
- *How does this encourage you?*

Paul first describes his death to the law – he is no longer under its authority (Romans 7:2, 4, 6). He uses this image to show how there is a complete, once for all, change. Romans 6:3-4, 6 also uses this imagery of identifying with Christ in his death; so close is our union with Christ by the Holy Spirit that Chris's death, life, resurrection, and righteousness is ours.

Paul triumphantly speaks of living by faith in Christ and having Christ live in him. His personality is not negated; rather, Paul is now truly free to be Paul and who God created him to be. His power source has changed. He now lives by the power of Jesus' Spirit, who lives in him (see also Romans 8:9-11). The law demanded, but Jesus gave – his own life for salvation, and his own life for living a godly life.

d. Based on verse 21, how might a person "set aside the grace of God"? What would be the result?

- *What is grace? How does God demonstrate grace?*
- *Why is gaining righteousness through the law opposed to grace?*
- *If we could earn God's favor, was Christ's death necessary?*
- *What two means of salvation are directly opposed to each other?*
- *How do verses 20-21 summarize Paul's argument?*

Paul clarifies setting aside the grace of God right in the verse: it is gaining righteousness by trying to follow the law. This approach says in effect, "God, I do not need grace. I do not believe that Jesus' death was really payment enough for my sin. And I think that I am capable of keeping the law well enough to earn at least part of my salvation that way." Paul's logic is clear: Why should the Son of God have suffered the agony of the cross and given his life if people could find salvation on their own by keeping the law?

Verses 20-21 summarize Paul's argument. Law and grace as ways of salvation are opposed to each other. We die to self-efforts, and rely on God's grace by faith in Christ. Christ's righteousness is our own (2 Corinthians 5:21). Thus, we are saved and are given the power to live righteously. We are saved by God's grace through faith in Jesus and live righteously by faith because we died with Christ and Christ lives in us. The law can do neither. So what is the role of the law? Paul will explain that as the letter goes on.

Discovering Our Stories

a. Paul speaks of dying to the law and living by faith in Christ. What does this look like in daily life?

- *What is God laying on your heart? What might he be calling you to this week?*

b. What do you think Paul's confrontation with Peter can teach believers about inclusion in God's family? About discrimination? How are we called to act on that?

c. What is your next step as a result of this study?

d. Read Psalm 103 as a praise for God's grace of righteousness.

More to Discover

Question 2a | 2 Corinthians 12:12; Galatians 3:5 (signs of God's work)

2c | Psalm 125; Isaiah 25:4; 41:17; James 1:27; 2:5 (God's concern for the poor)

3 | Acts 10 (used to eat with Gentiles)
Luke 22:54-62 ("afraid of those")

4a | Ephesians 2:11-14; Galatians 3:26-28 (Jew and Gentile)

4b | John 14:6 (way of salvation)
Romans 13:10; Galatians 5:6, 14 (fulfillment of the law)

4c | Romans 7:2, 4, 6 (died to the law)
Romans 6:3-4, 6 (crucified with Christ)
Romans 8:9-11 (Christ lives in me)

4d | Corinthians 5:21 (gaining righteousness)

3 Galatians 3:1-14
Faith or Law?

Optional Share Question

What are some "unwritten rules" you observe in your household?

This remains a get-to-know-you question, while still introducing the purposes of "law" in our families. You could lead the group to a discussion of unwritten society rules, and the pressure we feel when we enter into situations where there are many unwritten rules. Law always brings pressure, both good and bad.

Getting Started

In chapter 2, Paul establishes his authority and gospel: "a person is not justified by the works of the law, but by faith in Jesus Christ" (2:16). Can the Galatians not see the truth of the gospel from their own experience? Yet, Paul knows that the false teachers will also have a response, drawing from the Old Testament. Can the Galatians not see the truth of the gospel from the Old Testament? In this lesson, we will discover together with the early Christians the experience and history of the gospel.

Discovering Together

1. Galatians 3:1-5

Glossary: cross of Christ, flesh, law, miracles, Holy Spirit

a. What have the Galatians experienced? What does this say about their salvation?

- *What do they know about Jesus?*
- *How was Jesus "clearly portrayed as crucified" before their "very eyes"? How might the audiences in Acts 13:26-29 and in 1 Corinthians 1:23 see Christ crucified?*

- *How do they experience the Spirit?*
- *What does God do to confirm their faith in verse 5?*
- *How does this show their salvation to be genuine?*
- *How does your testimony also point to the truth of your salvation?*

Paul reminds the Galatians of what they experienced. They heard the gospel preached, they received the Spirit (Acts 13:52), and see God work miracles (Acts 14:3, 8-10, 19-20). All this is by faith in Jesus. Paul asks a series of rhetorical questions for emphasis, knowing the Galatians know the answers because they should be obvious to any believer.

The believers truly saw Jesus crucified through Paul's preaching, as they were not present at the crucifixion. This is the power of the Word! Acts 13:26-39 or 1 Corinthians 1:23 may be helpful.

Group members may have diverse views on miracles. Do not let your group become distracted by the topic of miracles. Paul mentions them as one of the signs that they were truly saved.

To help your group connect, you may consider some of the following questions:

- *Why might it easy for the Galatians to sway from the truth so quickly?*
- *Why are people tempted to "do more" for salvation?*
- *What might the Galatians fear getting wrong? How might a Galatian Christian respond to Paul? "Well, Paul, we thought..."*

The Galatians are not alone in their swiftness to sway from the truth. The Galatians face external pressures from the Judaizers and false teaching. Perhaps there are also internal pressures: the human desire for self-effort, pride, independence, to prove ourselves, or to cover shame. Your group members also face external and internal pressures. They may be tempted to add flesh to the Holy Spirit's work – either through the high of self-effort, or the low of feeling they are a big enough sinner they need to do more to cover up.

b. What do the Galatians receive in verses 2, 5? How? (see also v. 14)

- *Who is the Holy Spirit? Who gives the Holy Spirit?*
- *How might the Holy Spirit have been involved in the beginning of their faith? What does it mean to begin by the Holy Spirit? How might Titus 3:4-7 help us understand?*

- *Why is the Holy Spirit such a special gift?*
- *Who can receive the Holy Spirit?*
- *What do we learn about God? How willing is he to give us gifts, and to confirm his work?*

God gave them the Holy Spirit. Not by reward, not by some superior moral achievement, but to each Galatian believer through faith in Jesus. With these signs of the Spirit's work among them, the early Christians have assurance that God receives them as his children through faith in Christ. The Holy Spirit is the evidence of their salvation (Acts 2:38; 2 Corinthians 1:21-22). Isaiah said it would be a sign of God's restoration (Isaiah 44:4), which Christ has brought. The Spirit is God himself, indwelling us. What greater gift could we receive?

c. What comfort can we take from the promise of the Holy Spirit?

d. How are the Galatians "trying to finish"? Why is Paul frustrated with the Galatian believers?

- *What are two ways Paul contrasts here?*
- *How are we to finish our Christian walk? How does Paul live his life in Galatians 2:20-21? Where does he get the power for his Christian walk?*
- *Does God save us and then leave us to be good people on our own? How does Paul indicate that God helps us after salvation as well? (Philippians 1:6; 2:12-13)*

In verse 3, Paul asks, if salvation is given to them by faith – why are works of the law necessary now? The Galatians are trying to finish by their own works. It should be clear to your group that there are two exclusive ways. One either follows law and self-effort, or faith in Jesus. Praise be to God that he does not just give us a new, clean start and then ask us to do better. Christ lives in us, and we live by faith in the Son of God. God works in us as we keep in step with the Holy Spirit (Galatians 5:25).

You could begin to collect a list of words that characterize each way, adding to the lists in each lesson. Paul will elaborate. One list could have law, flesh, slavery, sin, death; the other list could have grace, faith, Holy Spirit, inheritance, promise, freedom, sonship, righteousness, life.

If your group wonders, you may use questions to help see that "foolish" here means gullible or unperceptive, not naturally stupid. "Bewitched" carries the sense of being blinded by magic, which is all the more bewildering to Paul when those same Galatian eyes once were focused on Jesus.

2. Galatians 3:6 (read also Genesis 15:1-6)

Glossary: Abraham (Abram), righteous

> **Whom does Paul introduce as an example at this point? Why might Abraham be important to the Judaizers?**

Genesis 15:1-6 adds important information.

- *What is God's promise to Abraham in Genesis 15?*
- *How does Abraham respond to God?*
- *How does God respond to Abraham as a result of his faith in God? How does Abraham gain a right standing with God?*
- *What parallels might Paul draw to the Galatian controversy? How is righteousness gained? How do both show faith in God? How does God respond to their faith in him?*
- *What do you learn about God? How does he respond to us?*

Paul introduces Abraham. Be sensitive to newcomers who do not know Abraham and his role in Jewish history. Refer to the glossary if necessary. Judaizers refer back to Abraham to support their arguments. Paul uses their own argument against them: Abraham received righteousness not by circumcision (Genesis 17), but by faith (Genesis 15:6).

God promised countless descendants to Abraham and his wife Sarah. Yet, they were childless. Even though God's promise seemed impossible, Abraham trusted in the Promise-Giver. God counted his faith as righteousness.

Use questions to draw the many parallels out between Abraham and the Galatians. Both had faith in God. Their faith is counted as righteousness, which comes ultimately from the saving work of Christ. Commentator Alan Cole notes:

> Abraham, like the Galatians, had believed God, trusted God's word – and God accepted that faith, that trust.... Abraham entered into his particular blessing by realizing that he could

do nothing himself, confessing it to God, and throwing himself on God, counting on God to do what he could not. That is the paradox of faith, as true for us as for Abraham. It was by ceasing to try to do anything for himself, and by accepting this position of humble and utter dependence, that Abraham was "justified."

3. Galatians 3:7-9

Glossary: blessing, faith, gospel

a. Who does Paul say are the true "children of Abraham"?

- *Who are the biological children of Abraham? Why might they take pride in that?*
- *What new kind of "descendants" does Paul recognize? What distinguishes the true child of Abraham?*
- *How does this blessing come through one of Abraham's descendants, Jesus, to all people, Jew and Gentile alike?*
- *Whom does God want to bless? Whom does God want the gospel to go to? What do you see about God's heart for the world?*

Paul says the true children of Abraham are not biological, but spiritual. The Jews attach great importance to the fact that they are the biological descendants of Abraham, who is revered as the one who received God's promise of blessing. They assume that this blessing is passed on to them because they are his physical descendants.

Yet, blessing comes through a right standing with God, and that is not biological or by the law, but by faith in Jesus Christ, Abraham's descendant. Abraham's right standing with God was because he believed in God's promises. Abraham's family is a family of faith, not of genealogy. Romans 4:18-25 is a beautiful description of Abraham's faith in God, which might be worth exploring with your group.

From the beginning, God's redemptive plan for humankind included all nations. In fact, in Genesis 12:3, God speaks to Abraham and promises that all peoples on earth will be blessed through him (see also Isaiah 2:2 for another example).

b. What do you think was the gospel ("good news") announced to Abraham?

- *What is the essence of the gospel? How do you see that in Genesis 15:1-6?*
- *How do we understand the gospel more clearly now, after Jesus?*
- *What questions do you have?*

The complete gospel (1 Corinthians 15:1-4) was not clearly shared to Abraham, as that is about Jesus ("God's Story" at the beginning of the book will clarify the time for new group members). However, the essence of the gospel is that we are saved by grace through faith in Jesus and not by works or circumcision (Ephesians 2:8-9). Abraham also knew he was saved by grace through faith in God. Old Testament believers and New Testament believers are saved by the same means. Abraham did not know Jesus, but he believed the promise. The salvation is still, always, by grace through faith in the finished work of Christ, whether that is belief in the promise (Abraham) or belief in the accomplished work (us).

Be sensitive to the Holy Spirit's work among your group members. Some of them may have questions at this point. Allow sufficient time so as not to rush through this part of the lesson.

c. Who is blessed? What does it mean to be blessed?

- *How does one receive the blessing promised to all people through Abraham? Can we receive it by keeping the law? By being of Jewish lineage? What is the single requirement? How did Abraham's life exemplify this quality?*
- *What does it mean to be blessed?*
- *How might the Galatians feel upon hearing this verse?*
- *What would it be like to be assured of God's blessing? OR How do you enjoy God's blessing?*

The blessing is available to all nations through faith in Jesus (Ephesians 1:3). The glossary may help your group understand blessing, as it can be a word with various understandings. It is enjoying the favor of God – and all else flows from that. Abraham had many struggles and sins, but he enjoyed the blessing of God. This may be a time to pause and celebrate God's blessing on us, or for newcomers to explore what it might mean to be assured of God's blessing. It is through Christ – even for those who struggle.

Specific blessings your group members may suggest could include the benefit of belonging to God, being accepted and loved by him, having one's sins forgiven through Christ, knowing that God always listens to and protects and guides his people, or the gift of the Spirit.

4. Galatians 3:10-14

Glossary: Book of the Law, curse, justification, redeem

a. How does Paul describe those who rely on the works of the law, and why?

- *How many of the laws in the Book of the Law does someone have to follow in order to be saved by the law?*
- *How are the Galatians coming again under the curse? Are they (or is anyone) able to keep the law perfectly?*
- *Why might Paul quote from Deuteronomy 27:26? How might the Judaizers use the Old Testament?*
- *What has God provided in verse 9 by faith in Jesus? What are the contrasts you see between verse 9 and 10?*
- *What would it look like to come under or rely on the law today?*

Those who rely on their own ability to follow the law are under a curse, for no one can keep the law perfectly. Paul focuses his argument here again on the Old Testament, which the Judaizers rely on. This time he quotes Deuteronomy 27:26 which refers to a curse on anyone who does not keep all of the law (James 2:10). There is a contrast between blessing through faith in Christ, and curse through the law. Why would anyone want to return to a way that would only lead to a curse? God has made the way to blessing!

Be sensitive to your group; make sure all understand the terms.

Some members may question how God can be a God of love and yet "curse" those who do not keep the law perfectly. To not keep the law is a violation of good; it is sin, falling short of God's standard (Romans 3:23). This demands justice, or a curse of separation from a holy God or judgment. Nor is this unloving. God is love, and thus he works for good. He comes in judgment against all that is against good. Thus, in love he seeks justice, which is the curse here. Lawbreakers (all of us) place ourselves under the curse by disobedience. Yet, God is merciful, and so Jesus became that curse.

b. What is the difference between observing the law and living by faith in verses 11-12?

- *Which one can justify?*
- *Which one leads to life and blessing, and why?*
- *What is the law not based on? How does the second half of verse 12 show what it is based on?*
- *Whom does one rely on when doing the works of the law? Whom does one rely on when living by faith in Jesus?*
- *In your own words, summarize what we learned about faith.*

Those who observe the law live by the law (Leviticus 18:4-5), but the righteous live by faith in Jesus Christ (Habakkuk 2:4). The issue is the power for life. As Galatians 2:19-20 and Colossians 3:4 says, Christ is our life. He is our power for living.

Law	Faith in Jesus
. . . cannot justify (v. 11)	. . . justifies us (v. 11)
. . . does not lead to righteousness (v. 11)	. . . leads to righteousness (v. 11)
. . . not based on faith in Jesus, but based on self-effort and works (v. 12)	. . . based on Jesus and his work (v. 12)

"Living by faith" can be a very new concept to some members. You may choose some of these questions to explore:

- *How will the righteous live? What does it mean to "live by faith"?*
- *What is Paul urging his readers to put their faith in?*
- *Name some specific instances in daily life. What would it look like to live by faith, that is, to place your whole hope and trust on Jesus in that situation?*
- *When we fail with the law, where can we go with our failures? Does the law provide a solution to our failure? How does the law highlight our failures?*
- *When we fail under grace, having placed all our hope for right living in Jesus, where can we go with our failures? How will God receive us in Christ? How does God help us overcome our failures?*

It may also be helpful to again clarify what faith is: it is not just the sincerity of our belief, but it is the object of our faith. We can have very sincere faith that a chair can hold us up, but if it is broken, it does not matter the sincerity of our faith. The object matters.

Living by faith means that is the way that life through Christ comes. "To live by faith" shows that faith is what one's whole way of life is oriented toward. Galatians 2:19-20 is an illustration of living by faith: Paul places his whole hope, his whole trust, squarely on Jesus.

The law responds to our guilt by judging our actions. It cannot respond to our faith; it can only condemn. It cannot provide a way out when we fail. We just condemn ourselves, and have nowhere to go except our own works again. With faith, we can run to Jesus who has covered it, and find the Father's embrace, and the Holy Spirit's power to live differently (Titus 2:11-14).

c. **What did Christ's death accomplish? What does that have to do with the curse of the law?**

- *How did Jesus take the curse of the law upon himself? Since he had kept the law perfectly, did he deserve such a death? Who does deserve this punishment? For whom was Jesus acting as a substitute?*
- *How did you experience that curse?*
- *What do you learn about Jesus? Why would he willingly become a curse?*
- *What does it mean to be redeemed?*

Jesus Christ redeemed us (see glossary). Jesus Christ took our place on the cross, taking upon himself our judgment and completely satisfying the demands of the law in perfect obedience (if your group needs help understanding he perfectly fulfilled God's requirements, see Matthew 5:17, 20; 2 Corinthians 5:21; 1 John 3:5). In God's eyes, Jesus became a curse – placing himself under God's judgment by taking on all our sin. As guilty sinners, we deserve to die – to suffer the curse to pay the penalty for our own sins. But as Paul writes clearly in 2 Corinthians 5:21: "God made him [Jesus Christ] who had no sin to be sin for us, so that in him we might become the righteousness of God." By becoming a curse, Jesus fulfilled the promise made to Abraham that all nations would be blessed through him (v. 8).

To personalize the conversation, you may adapt the following questions to your group:

- What does it mean to you that someone would die for you, for you personally?
- How would you like to respond to the Most High, the most Glorious King, who gave himself for you?
- How have you felt the pressure of the law? The pressure, guilt, or shame of shortcomings and failure? What hope does grace give you? What does it mean to be accepted and loved even in the midst of your guilt and this pressure?
- What is righteousness? What does it mean to have Christ be your righteousness?

Pray that the Holy Spirit will be working in your members' hearts so that they will clearly see the message of God's love and acceptance through Jesus Christ and his offer of freedom from the bondage of the law. If you feel your group would benefit, discuss the pressure that those who live under the law feel.

You may also choose to include an activity celebrating the fact that Christ did become a curse for us. This could be imagining the burden of the curse being placed on Christ, and then turning to one another with the simple statement, "You are blessed in Christ." Or coming to a physical cross at the place where you meet, and placing all we would like to leave there, and picking up a flower or something that symbolizes the blessing of God.

The promise of the Holy Spirit was discussed earlier; revisit it if you think it would benefit your group. It is a rich topic!

Discovering Our Stories

a. **Reflect on what we learned about Jesus Christ and what he has done. Personalize it. How would you like to respond to him?**

b. **What kind of pressure might the Galatians feel living under the law? Are there ways you feel or used to feel this pressure? What freedom is promised here? How are you being prompted to respond?**

c. **What is your next step as a result of this study?**

d. **Read Psalm 130 as a celebration of God's promised redemption.**

More to Discover

Question 1a | Acts 13:26-29; 1 Corinthians 1:23 (Christ portrayed as crucified)

Acts 13:52 (receive the Spirit)

Acts 14:3, 8-10, 19-20 (miracles)

1b | Isaiah 44:4; Acts 2:38; 2 Corinthians 1:21-22; Titus 3:4-7 (begin by the Spirit)

1d | Philippians 1:6; 2:12-13 (God's help to finish)

2 | Genesis 17 (circumcision)

3a |Genesis 12:3; Isaiah 2:2 (all nations will be blessed)

Romans 4:18-25 (Abraham's faith)

3b |1 Corinthians 15:1-4; Ephesians 2:8-9 (the gospel)

3c | Ephesians 1:3 (blessing)

4a | Deuteronomy 27:26; Romans 3:23; James 2:10 (cursed is everyone)

4b | Leviticus 18:4-5 (live by the law)

Habakkuk 2:14; Colossians 3:4; Titus 2:11-14 (live by faith)

4c | Matthew 5:17, 20; 2 Corinthians 5:21; 1 John 3:5 (Jesus' fulfilment of the law in our place)

4 Galatians 3:15-4:7
Sons, Not Slaves!

Optional Share Question

Have you ever inherited a valuable item? How did receiving the gift make you feel toward the one who gave it to you?

This share question will help prepare the way for the discussion of inheritance at the end. What a gift we have received in Jesus!

Getting Started

Paul continues to discuss faith in Jesus versus works. In the last lesson, Paul drew from the experience of the Galatians and Abraham, as well as from the law. In this section, Paul looks further at the Old Testament, where God formed a relationship based on promise to his people. Yet, God also gave his people the law. What is the role of the law? Paul says it has a role – but Paul invites the Galatians, and us, to consider how we relate to God now in Christ.

Additional Note to the Leader: You (and your group) may feel that Paul is too repetitious in his frequent statements defending the gospel of salvation by faith. However, ask your group to compare it to a precious gem. To glance at it only once from one perspective is to miss the many-faceted splendor of the stone. But when it is studied in detail from many angles and in different lights, its full beauty is revealed. In Galatians Paul polishes the gem of "faith alone" until all else pales in comparison. As you come to a greater awareness of the beauty of this truth, your enthusiasm and renewed appreciation will inevitably be communicated to those who study it with you.

Discovering Together

1. Galatians 3:15-18

Glossary: Abraham, covenant, grace, Jesus Christ, law, seed

a. What example does Paul use to demonstrate the difference between the law and the promise? What do we learn about the nature of the promise from Paul's example?

- *How is a last will similar to the promise? Could anything set aside a human covenant? Can anything set aside God's promise?*
- *What assurance does this give the Galatians? Us?*
- *To whom was the promise given?*
- *Who gave the promises?*
- *To how many people would the promise come through?*
- *What descendant (or "seed") of Abraham was directly involved in this covenant?*
- *What was Jesus Christ's role in the covenant?*
- *How was Christ's coming and death related to the promise given to Abraham?*

Paul uses the example of a human covenant. This is familiar for his readers, but it is not as immediately obvious to us today. The study note will help. Like a last will, so it was with the inheritance God promised to Abraham. God gave the inheritance through a promise, and those who received it would do so by believing that promise. Nothing could replace that covenant of promise – not even the law.

God spoke the promises to Abraham (Galatians 3:8; Genesis 12:1-3; 15:5-6). (Be sensitive to anyone who was not present in the last lesson, and use the glossary and review questions if necessary to refresh everyone's mind on who Abraham is.) The promise is another word for the blessings spoken of in the previous lesson. Yet, Paul emphasizes that there was one offspring (or seed) through whom all the promises would come. That "seed" was Jesus Christ.

Jesus Christ is the most significant offspring of Abraham, the one who makes the inheritance by faith possible to all who believe in him (v. 16). You may want to refer back to verses 13 and 14, but do not spend too much time on this question, since it will be addressed in several other passages as well. Most commentators agree that Paul in other places uses a plural form of the word "seed," unlike the singular form he uses here, to refer to many descendants (v. 29, for example).

Study Note: The "human covenant" Paul writes of was similar to a last will and testament. Once such a legal document was drawn up, nothing could change it or replace it. The promised inheritance would come through this covenant and through nothing else.

b. What does the inheritance depend on? What does it not depend on?

- When was the law given according to this passage? Which came first?
- Does the law set aside the promise? Was it given to do the same thing as the promise?
- How does the example of a covenant help us understand verse 17?
- How does Galatians 3:14 help us understand what the inheritance is?
- Why does Paul mention God's grace in connection with the promise?
- What do you learn about God's character? Why might he give the promise based on grace?

The inheritance was based on the promise of God to Abraham and his descendants; like a covenant, not even the law could supersede it.

Focus the discussion on Paul's main point: the law was not given to replace the covenant of faith as a means to gain the promised salvation. The promise to Abraham came first (the Abrahamic covenant; Genesis 12-17), and then the law (Mosaic covenant; Exodus 19 and forward) ("God's Story" may be helpful). Like a last will, what comes later cannot set aside the promise. It could not be changed. Galatians 3:14 clarifies that the inheritance here is the blessing.

It is important for your group to discover God's grace as well. The inheritance was a gift of grace, God's unmerited favor. It did not depend on anything Abraham had done, nor on keeping the law.

To summarize, commentator S. J. Mikolaski writes:

> If the inheritance now comes by law, promise and faith are canceled. However, God gave the blessing to Abraham by promise and faith. This does not undercut the validity of law, nor is the law to be regarded as a codicil which displaces promise, because law is not the condition of receiving the promise.

2. Galatians 3:19-25

Glossary: angel, faith, sin, transgression, righteousness

a. What is the purpose of the law? (vv. 19, 24)

- *What might the law reveal to us about transgression? How might Romans 7:7 help us understand this?*
- *How does the law show us God's character?*
- *How would an awareness of one's sin and one's inability to keep the law perfectly also increase one's awareness of the need for the salvation offered through Christ? How might the law lead us to Christ, in verse 24?*
- *Was the law ever intended as a means to gain God's inheritance or to life? What was it intended to do?*
- *Are humans able to keep the law perfectly according to James 2:10? How might that point us to our need for Jesus?*
- *Is the law opposed to the promise? (v. 21) How might it help us understand the promise?*

Keeping the big picture in mind may be helpful: Paul is explaining to the Galatians the relationship between the covenant of faith and the law. The law does not replace or overshadow the covenant. So what is the purpose of the law? Your group members may be asking the same question. If so, that is a sign that they have been following Paul's argument closely and are thinking it through. The law is given to show us the way to live, to teach us good – and to show us how we continually fail. It points us to the promise, to faith in Christ.

The additional note to the leader following the "Historical Snapshot" also may provide support for any questions on the relationship of the law to believers.

As the discussion moves to verse 19, you may consider using some of the following quesitons. It may help to read verse 19 in different translations; the NLT or Amplified may help clarify. The Tyndale commentary notes that the law does not make us holy but awakens us to sin. Romans 3:20; 4:15; or 7:7 may help show how the law pointed out sin; and James 2:10 says that making even one error means we have broken all of it. The law shows we are guilty, which should point us to the promise.

- What does the word "added" in verse 19 show us about the relationship of the law to the promise?
- How have the false teachers among the Galatians distorted this relationship between law and faith?
- Do people still distort that relationship today?

"Added" shows that the law was only an additional element that is intended to work with, not replace or oppose, the covenant of faith established by the promise. God's relationship with his people was by promise and grace. The false teachers put law, rather than promise, back at the center of our relationship with God.

Verse 20 is a minor point, but continues the argument that the promise is superior to the law:

- How did God give the law?
- How did God give the promise to Abraham in Genesis 12:1 and 15:1, 4?
- Which of these carries more weight – God's direct revelation or a revelation brought through several go-betweens?

Paul seems to be saying that the law was given through angels to a mediator (Moses); it was not direct revelation. However, the promise came directly from God to Abraham.

Study Note: Jewish tradition held that God gave his law to Moses, an Old Testament leader, through the angels. Moses acted as mediator between God and the people of Israel (Galatians 3:19), pleading their cause before God and teaching God's law to the people (Acts 7:38; Deuteronomy 33:2).

b. What is the condition of the entire world? What is the only thing that can change that condition? (v. 22)

- What is in control?
- How do Romans 11:32, or Romans 3:9 help us understand this?

Verse 22 shows that we are imprisoned by sin. Scripture shows us our sin, and we ourselves are powerless to escape (Romans 3:9; 5:6; 6:6-7). But there is hope, for freedom and the promise comes through faith in Christ our Savior.

Some in your group may object to the idea that sin rules over them, or have a false picture of God turning some people over to sin as a master. Rather, humankind chose to be slaves to sin in the garden as they sought independence from God (Romans 5:12-14, 18-19). We have all chosen sin over God. The basic sin nature can be seen even in two infants fighting over one toy. Yet, despite our sinfulness, God chose us and died for us.

c. What image does Paul use to describe people's lives under the law before Christ came? What does this image suggest about the law?

- *What feelings does this image provoke?*
- *In Genesis 17:7 and Jeremiah 31:31-34, what kind of relationship did God promise his people? How does this seem to compare with the relationship here?*

Paul speaks of us being in custody, locked up. Some group members may feel a sense of oppression, lack of freedom, a feeling of darkness and confinement. Help your group to see that that is part of what Paul was trying to convey to his readers. Genesis 17:7 and Jeremiah 31:31-34 show a close relationship that God desired, and promised. They were not to be slaves to sin, but God's people.

d. How is one released from the law's "supervision"?

- *What new image for the law does Paul use? What does that image convey about our previous relationship to the law?*
- *How has the believer's relationship to the law changed?*
- *What happened so that we no longer need the law in that way?*

Christ has now come and completed his saving work on our behalf; this part of redemptive history is complete so our relationship to the law has changed.

Paul's language in verse 24 conveys a less stern image of the law: that of a trusted guardian (similar to governess or nanny) who watches over young children. The law served a purpose for a time, but there comes a time for maturity – just as in the life of a growing child. Faith changes our relationship to the law, and to God. "Now that faith has come" there is no longer a need for the law to serve as a tutor for believers.

3. Galatians 3:26-29
Glossary: baptize, Gentiles

a. What is the identity of those who believe? What is the contrast from the verses above?

- *How completely has one's identity changed through faith? (See also Galatians 2:19-20.)*
- *Why is baptism a significant part of that change?*

There has to be a clean break, Paul emphasizes, between life under the law's supervision and the new life of faith in Christ. The son or daughter of God takes on a completely new identity. In 2 Corinthians 5:17, Paul calls us a "new creation" in Christ (also Ephesians 4:24).

Baptism is a sign of our union with Christ as believers. Be careful here not to become mired in a discussion of the various methods of baptism and denominational differences on the subject. Have your group work with the basic definition given in the glossary. Romans 6:3-4 may be a helpful reference here.

b. What does Paul say about those who belong to Christ in verses 28 and 29? Why might this have been important for the church in Galatia, and for us today?

- *How might conditions in Paul's day differ from the unity Paul describes here? How does the study note help us understand this?*
- *What is the basis of one's standing before God? How does the life Christ gives change human ways of making distinctions between people?*
- *How might this new perspective affect one's relationship with others?*
- *What do you learn about God and his desire for unity in his people? Why might that be important to God?*

Paul makes it clear that we are all one in Christ. We are all heirs. The human distinctions we sometimes make based on gender, ethnicity, etc., have no bearing on our salvation. We are all Abraham's seed. The Galatian church is likely a mixture of Jews and Gentiles, slave and free, men and women. They are examples of inequality in society, but in Christ the inequality is gone and we are one. Jesus Christ is our only standing before God. No ethnicity, race, social status, or any works of ours can earn any more righteousness. We are all equal, therefore.

This has great implications for how we treat others. This verse does not mean, however, that there are no distinctions from an earthly standpoint. We are uniquely diverse, and can celebrate our various different ethnicities, and our unique genders. A Jew in Christ can be a Jew; a Nigerian in Christ can be a Nigerian; a Korean in Christ can be a Korean; a Greek in Christ can be a Greek. We celebrate our distinct cultural identities as showing different facets of God and his creativity, but our different identities do not give us reason to be prideful over another group.

You may also talk about what it means to be an heir to the promise (v. 29).

- Who are Abraham's "seed"? Is Paul speaking of biological descendants here?
- How does this verse relate to 3:14?
- In what sense does the believer belong to Christ?
- How does it encourage you to belong to Christ?

We are all heirs, and Abraham's seed (descendants). While Christ may be the one seed, we are now in him and through him part of Abraham's family of faith. Belonging to Christ recognizes he has redeemed us (Galatians 3:14), and is our Master and Savior.

Study Note: The three distinctions Paul mentions here were part of the daily fabric of society and the Jewish religious tradition. Jewish law discriminated between male and female, slave and free, Jew and Gentile. Jewish males were accustomed to giving thanks each day that they were neither female nor Gentile.

4. Galatians 4:1-5

Glossary: elemental spiritual forces of the world, redeem, sons

a. To what does Paul compare life under the law?

- What does Paul imply here again about the role of the law? About the need to become heirs?
- Following this analogy, how would the life of faith differ from life under the law?
- How might the basic principles of religious experience (the law for Jews, the superstitions and rites of idol worship for Gentiles) hold people in slavery?

Those who live under the law are like small children who are not yet old enough to participate fully in governing the family estate. They really have no more freedom and responsibility than do the slaves on the estate There is need for maturity – not the growth we do, but the new era of faith that Christ brings. The life of faith is a life of blessing, inheritance, of reaching fullness in Christ.

The religious principles of law or rite have no place for faith in Jesus Christ. They are built around what a person can do to gain favor with God.

b. What event changes the believer's status from that of a child to that of a son? What new information does Paul add?

- *What does it mean that Christ came when the set time had fully come? What does that say about God's plan?*
- *How does this relate to the analogy in verse 2?*
- *Why was it necessary for Christ to be born of a woman and also born under the law?*
- *How might we need a human representative to redeem us and pay our debt? Why couldn't any sinful human have to do that? Why did the representative redeemer have to perfectly fulfill the law?*
- *How much does our relationship to him mean to God? How much does our freedom mean to God?*
- *What do you learn about God?*

Paul makes it clear that Christ's life and death changes the status for those who put their faith in him. Verse 4 speaks of the time God had set for his people's coming to maturity, out from under the law's supervision. God knew the perfect time (Ephesians 1:5-10).

Be sensitive to group member's knowledge of Christ. Only one who was fully human and who kept the demands of the law perfectly could bear the punishment of all those who had failed to keep the law (see also 1 Peter 2:22-24). In order to pay the debt, someone needed to be born under the law and fulfill the law. Yet, every single human is a debtor and unable to fulfil the law. So, Christ took on flesh, and was born of a woman. He perfectly kept the law in our place as one under the law. Then, he exchanged his righteousness for our sin. Only a God-man could do all this. His humanity was essential to his paying our debt.

As the discussion shifts to our identity, consider questions such as the following to bring the discussion deeper:

- *What benefits does a son have that a slave does not have?*
- *What might it mean to "receive the full rights of sons" (4:5)?*
- *Do we have all those rights now?*

Those who are not natural heirs by reason of biological descent from Abraham acquire the status of sonship through faith in Jesus Christ. Your group may name a few differences in legal standing for the believer who is a son or heir with full rights of sons and a person who is yet in spiritual slavery. For example, we have the blessing (Galatians 3:14; Ephesians 1:3). We have bold access to the Father (v. 6; Ephesians 3:12). We experience this to a degree now, but yet we will experience the fullness of this inheritance when Christ comes again (1 Peter 1:3-6).

5. Galatians 4:6-7

Glossary: Abba

a. What does Paul tell his readers about the Spirit?

- *What does this passage say about belonging in God's family?*
- *What is one of the main works of the Holy Spirit in a believer's life? What does his presence accomplish in the heart?*
- *What does the cry of "Abba" tell us about the relationship between God and his adopted children?*
- *What do you learn about God's character? What does he want our relationship with him to be like?*
- *How are you crying out, "Abba," in your life? How do you enjoy that relationship?*

The Holy Spirit dwells in us (1 Corinthians 6:19; 2 Corinthians 1:22) and makes us God's child, experiencing his love and intimacy (Romans 5:5). The glossary will help your group understand the intimate experience we can have with God!

b. Based on your study thus far, how do you think the Galatians have denied their sonship?

- *How does a relationship with God by the Holy Spirit contrast with what the false teachers are trying to promote? How do the demands of the law undermine the relationship of love and trust between parent and child?*

The Galatians revert to works, working as slaves. They are following a cold set of laws, legalism. They are not enjoying the grace-filled ability to run to God and cry, Abba!

Be sensitive to the fact that for newcomers who rebelled against legalistic Christianity or who may have a stereotyped image of Christianity as a list of do's and don'ts, this may be a refreshing, but perhaps confusing new insight. Encourage them to taste the joy of freedom in Christ, to see Christianity as a relationship to be nurtured rather than an obligation to be paid.

Discovering Our Stories

a. What have you learned about being a child of God? How might this, or does this, impact your life?

- *In what specific circumstance does this give you encouragement?*

b. What do you think the image of "clothing yourselves with Christ" implies about the life of faith? (v. 27; Romans 13:14; Colossians 3:9-10)

- *How can you remind yourself you are clothed with Christ this week?*
- *What does this say about where your protection and covering comes from? How does this encourage you in your walk this week?*

This image speaks of change, and newness.

c. What is your next step as a result of this study?

d. Read Psalm 107:1-16. How does this celebrate God's redemption?

More to Discover

Question 1a | Genesis 12:1-3; 15:5-6 (promises spoken)
1b | Genesis 12-17 (covenant with Abraham)
  Exodus 19 (law given)
2a | Genesis 12:1; 15:1, 4 (God giving the promise)
  Deuteronomy 33:2; Acts 7:38 (giving of the law)
  Romans 3:20; 4:15; 7:7; James 2:10 (law and sin)
2b | Romans 3:9; 5:6; 6:6-7 (locked under sin)
  Romans 5:12-14, 18-19; James 1:14-15 (source of sin)
2c | Genesis 17:7; Jeremiah 31:31-34 (God's promised relationship)
3a | Ephesians 4:24; 2 Corinthians 5:17 (new identity)
  Romans 6:3-4 (baptism)
4b | Ephesians 1:5-10 (time had fully come)
  1 Peter 2:22-24 (to redeem)
  Ephesians 1:3-6; 3:12; 1 Peter 1:3-6 (sonship)
5a | Romans 5:5; 1 Corinthians 6:19; 2 Corinthians 1:22 (God sent the Spirit)

5 Galatians 4:8-31
A Pastor's Plea

Optional Share Question

Do you like admitting you are heading in the wrong directly or lost when you are driving? Why or why not?

This question will help introduce the lesson. Paul calls on the Galatians to admit that they are heading in the wrong direction. By lesson 5, you may find you no longer need to use warm up questions as group safety may be built up.

Getting Started

The Galatians are heading in the wrong direction – and Paul steps in and pleads for them to return. He uses a threefold appeal to the Galatians. First, Paul says they are free, but are now returning to slavery (vv. 8-11). Then he calls for a return of their trust in him and their close relationship, based on truth and freedom (vv. 12-20). Last, Paul appeals to history, saying that even the Jewish history mapped out the direction for freedom (vv. 21-31). As we study, how do you see God's concern for you?

Discovering Together

1. Galatians 4:8-11

Glossary: elemental spiritual forces, know

a. What are the Galatians "turning back to"? How does Paul describe their former way of life?

- *What was their status before turning to God? How might these early believers have been slaves to the gods they had worshiped?*
- *How might verse 10 help us understand elements of their slavery? In verse 10, what are the Judaizers encouraging the Galatians*

to observe? How might this and law-keeping be a form of slavery again?

- What do you think are some of the "weak and miserable forces" they are turning back to? How are these forces related to Galatians 4:3? What do the adjectives say about these forces?
- Why might returning to these forces be tempting for the Galatians?
- How does the living God contrast to the weak and miserable forces?

By turning to law, the Galatians are turning back to "weak and miserable forces," things that can not save but only enslave.

Before the Galatians heard the gospel of salvation in Christ, they worshiped beings they thought were gods. Why were they slaves? Partly due, as the study note says, to the regulations of worship trying to appease the gods. The gods, and fear of gods, controlled their lives. Also because they were slaves to sin apart from God (Romans 6:6, 16-17).

The Judaizers, false teachers, are apparently encouraging the Galatians to keep the religious festivals and special days of the Jews. Once again, they are relying on something other than Christ to earn favor with a deity. Rules, not faith in Jesus, are controlling their standing before God. These are the same forces of Galatians 4:3.

Study Note: Greeks and Romans worshiped many gods. Religious festivals, feast days, rituals, and sacrifices ordered the lives of those who worshiped these gods. They made sacrifices to ask for the god's blessing and to appease the gods.

Jews also had religious festivals, such as the Passover and Feast of Unleavened Bread, Feast of Weeks, and Feast of Booths. Special days included the weekly Sabbath (governed by many rules), and Yom Kippur ("Day of Atonement" in English).

b. **Why do you think Paul emphasizes the fact that God knows them?**

- When they were worshiping other gods, what was their relationship to God?
- What does it mean to know God? to be known by God?
- What does God's knowledge of them say about his role in redemption?
- How do you think knowing God and being known by him should have made a difference in the Galatians' lives?

- *How does it bring you comfort that God knows you?*
- *What do you learn about God and his role in salvation?*

The emphasis on being known by God shows his role in initiating redemption, and his love.

Knowing God and being known by God should help the Galatians discern truth. They have experienced God as Father (Galatians 3:1-5; 4:6-7). Believers can have a personal knowledge of God; yet we will never fully know him. God's knowledge of us is greater, deeper, and more comprehensive. This also refers to his role in salvation. His knowledge implies a choosing (John 13:18). He initiates the relaitonship. Yet the Galatians are trying to put other things in between. This passages emphasizes that their salvation is based on what Christ has done, not what they have done or will do. Christ's life and death are what redeem the Galatians.

It may also be fruitful to explore Paul's response:

- *What is Paul's reaction and concern?*
- *What do you imagine Paul's feelings were like at this point in time?*
- *What do you learn about a leader's heart?*

Paul fears that his "brothers and sisters" (3:15, 4:12), his beloved "children" (4:19) are slipping away from the true gospel. The young churches are very important to Paul, as well as Christ's honor. He is distraught to see this at stake.

2. Galatians 4:12-20

a. How would you describe Paul's former relationship with the Galatians? What words show the intensity of Paul's feelings for them?

- *How does Paul address them in verse 12? Why?*
- *How did the Galatians receive Paul at first? Why might they not have done so?*

Paul regards his readers as brothers and sisters (v. 12), members of the family of God. In spite of his illness (which we are unsure of what that is), which could have hindered a warm welcome, they welcomed him and were willing to do all they could for him.

If you have time, you may also discuss what you learn from Paul's method here.

- *What might Paul mean he "became like" them? How might 1 Corinthians 9:19-23 help us understand this?*
- *What do we learn from Paul's method of sharing the gospel?*
- *What does Paul urge them to do in return?*

Paul makes every effort to adapt to their culture and traditions as he presented the gospel of Christ to them. In return, he urges them to become like him – that is, like Christ and passionate about the true gospel (1 Corinthians 11:1). You might want to clarify with your group that Paul is not self-promoting; he is really asking them to become like Christ, who has completely changed Paul.

b. How does Paul describe the change in their relationship?

- *What word does Paul use to describe their relationship in verse 16?*
- *What is one of the things the false teachers are trying to do in verse 17?*
- *How forthright is Paul?*
- *What causes them to be enemies?*
- *Do you think this is an example of Ephesians 4:15? Why or why not?*
- *What motivates Paul to speak this way? What is his first concern, above all else?*
- *What do we learn about sharing truth?*

A once warm relationship is now described as being enemies, divided, alienated. The Judaizers want to alienate, and to direct the Galatians' zeal and loyalty toward them. Verse 15 reads differently in Bible translations. Some see it as an attitude of blessing toward Paul; others as a sense of their own blessedness or joy at their redemption ("blessed" in Romans 4:6-9; Galatians 3:9).

When the truth is at stake, Paul does not avoid confrontation. He is direct and forthright. You may choose to compare Paul's interaction with Peter (Galatians 2:11-14). He is speaking the truth in love (Ephesians 4:15). This is no soft, dilute "love" but a love that truly seeks the best for his readers. We see his love in his plea to them as children, and his desire to change his tone. This is painful for him as well.

Paul's first concern is the honor of Christ and the truth of the gospel. His authority to share the truth comes from no other source than Christ himself (Galatians 1:10). We also are called to share the truth in love, and in humility. We must also discern what is the core truth, and what are cultural, traditional, or personal preferences.

If helpful for your group, you could explore the motivations and zeal a bit further with questions such as:

- *How do both Paul and the Judaizers show zeal?*
- *How is Paul's motive different from the Judaizers?*
- *When is zeal a good attribute? For what purpose does Paul want his readers to be zealous? What does he imply about the constancy of their zeal?*
- *How might Paul's zeal be a reflection of God's zeal?*
- *What is your level of zeal toward the truth and others? How do you express that?*

Paul assures them that zeal is not bad – as long as it is directed toward the truth! (Romans 12:11) The Galatians apparently were very zealous for the gospel when Paul was among them. But after he left, their zeal flagged and they began to listen to "a different gospel" (Galatians 1:6).

c. What does Paul want for the Galatians? What does his imagery mean?

- *How does Paul shift his address in verse 19? What does this show about his relationship to them?*
- *What does Paul's goal tell us about the Christian life?*
- *What does Paul mean by the phrase "until Christ is formed in you"?*
- *What attributes of Christ might a believer reflect?*
- *How might this point to a deeper transformation? How might it be more than just copying Jesus?*
- *Who is zealous for Christ to be formed in you? For whom are you zealous to see that Christ is formed in them? What would this look like in daily life?*
- *What do you learn about the kind of relationship and life God wants? His work?*

He wants Christ to be "formed" in them; in other words, that the Galatians will grow and mature in Christ.

Paul addresses them as children; spiritually, he is their father and mother (1 Corinthians 4:15). Many in your group may be parents; mothers are familiar with the pain of childbirth, and they share the common concern that their children grow up to live strong and healthy lives. Paul uses the descriptive imagery of childbirth to describe his feelings.

For Christ to be formed in us shows that Christianity is not just rules; it is about a personal relationship with God. We are born again in his likeness (Romans 8:29; 2 Corinthians 3:18). It is not just about copying Christ, but having him as our life (Galatians 2:19-20; Colossians 3:4). Paul is anxious to see the evidence of Christian maturity in the lives of the Galatian believers (Ephesians 4:13, 15; Colossians 2:6-7.) Paul will unpack this further in Galatians chapter 5.

Groups may personalize the conversation as well – it is good that every believer has someone else pouring into them in order that Christ be formed in them, and that they too are pouring into someone else.

3. Galatians 4:21-27

Glossary: Abraham, covenant, flesh, Hagar, Isaac, Ishmael, Jerusalem, law, Mount Sinai, Sarah

a. To whom does Paul address this part of his letter? Why might his illustration have been particularly effective for them?

- *Where does this illustration come from? How might the Judaizers argue from the Old Testament?*
- *What might Paul say about their understanding of the law? Does Paul think that those "who want to be under the law" truly understand the law?*

Paul addresses those "who want to be under the law." He combats the heresy of the Judaizers, with an argument taken from the Jewish sacred writings, that is, the law. The glossary will help your group understand that the stories are part of "the law" as well. With a note of irony, Paul argues that though they want to be under the law, they do not understand the law.

b. Compare and contrast the two women and their offspring.

- *Who are Abraham and Sarah and Hagar?*
- *Whose son came by the flesh? What does it mean "according to the flesh"?*

- *Whose son came by promise? Whose promise was it?*
- *What is the status of Hagar and her offspring? Whom do she and her children represent?*
- *How are Mount Sinai and Jerusalem also symbols of life under the law?*
- *How is the free woman a symbol of grace and promise? If the free woman is the mother of believers, as verse 26 says, what is Paul emphasizing here?*
- *What does Paul mean by the Jerusalem that is above? How might Hebrews 12:22 and Revelation 21:2 help us understand this?*

To be sure that your group fully understands the relationship between Abraham, Sarah, and Hagar, you may want to read together Genesis 16:14 and 21:1-13 and consult the glossary. Your group members should understand that "the free woman" (v. 22) is Sarah. (Note: the Bible does not agree that having two wives, or having slaves, is okay. The Bible is realistic about what people did in those time periods, for better or for worse.)

The son of the slave woman (Ishmael by Hagar) was born "according to the flesh." Abraham showed a lack of faith in God by desiring to achieve something through his own actions. It was by human effort. The son of the free woman (Isaac by Sarah) was born of God's promise through divine means and is, therefore, of grace. You may wish to draw these out visually with word clusters. For instance, Hagar: slave, flesh, Mount Sinai, slaves, present Jerusalem. Sarah: free, divine promise, Jerusalem that is above, mother of believers.

The symbolic Hagar is a slave; she thus represents those under the law. Thus, she is associated with Mount Sinai, where the law was given, and the present Jerusalem, whose inhabitants still tried to live under the law (see the glossary). Those who try to get life by the law remain in bondage to the law.

The symbolic free woman represents the Jerusalem that is above. She is the mother of believers, because her offspring are by promise and grace. Hebrews 12:22 and Revelation 21:2 speak of a heavenly Jerusalem. In other words, it is the true spiritual capital. Only those who are born (or re-born) by grace can be free spiritually.

You may use these questions to summarize.

- *How do these two offspring symbolize the difference between salvation by faith in Christ and salvation based on obedience to the law?*

- *What difference does the promise make?*
- *Which group are you most living like? Do you rest in God's promise or are you still trying to earn his love in some way?*

The promise is the key difference. One is associated with slavery and bondage and efforts of the flesh; the other is associated with freedom because he is a child of promise.

You may choose to make these verses personal; be sensitive to those who are in your group. Many of us have a head knowledge of grace, but still find ourselves unsure of God's love and end up trying to prove ourselves in one way or another. Romans 5:5, 8; 1 John 3:1; 4:8-10, 19 are a few verses to just meditate on to assure ourselves of his love.

You may choose to explore some more of the original setting also:

- *Read John 8:33. How might Paul's argument be startling to Jews?*

Some groups may appreciate this optional question. The Judaizers would argue they are not slaves, and are descended from Abraham and Sarah. Paul is saying they are working by flesh, and thus are behaving/becoming like children of Hagar. "The stinging implication is that Jews who take pride in their natural descent from Abraham are really no better than Ishmael. The sons of grace are the true heirs of Abraham" (Mikolaski).

c. How does verse 27 continue the theme of promise?

- *Why is the barren woman to be glad?*
- *How can a barren woman have children? How does this show grace or promise?*
- *How many children does the woman in this verse have?*
- *How might this apply to the Galatians and the early church? (Galatians 3:7-8) How does the gathering of Gentiles into the church fulfill this promise? Is this still happening today? Do those who become Abraham's children by faith in Christ eventually outnumber those who are his natural descendants?*
- *What do you learn about God and his character?*

The barren woman is to rejoice because of the number of her children. A barren woman cannot have children – thus, these are divine gifts. The children of promise include Jews and Gentiles, slave and free, are numerous. God is lavish in his grace and promise.

You may ask groups to quickly sketch out the woman's joy. Or write a composite poem, where each member writes a line of joy or praise.

Paul applies this quote from Isaiah 54:1 to the New Testament church. Paul's use of this verse is beautifully complex. If your group has a good background knowledge of the Bible, it may be helpful to explore that a bit:

- How is this verse appropriate in connection with Sarah? What do you remember about her?
- This quotation is from Isaiah 54:1. Israel was in exile and God was promising restoration. How does Paul show that the church is the fulfillment of this promise? What does this add to our understanding?

In its original context, the verse did not refer to Sarah. Yet, the connection is clear: Sarah, the "mother" of those who would be heirs of Abraham through faith in God, had been barren for many years. Now, her children are numerous.

Paul is also indicating that, not only is the gospel of faith the fulfillment of the promise to Sarah and Abraham, but it is also the way God fulfills his promises of restoration after the exile. The ultimate return from exile is not Israel's physical return to her land; it is the saving work of Christ who restores us to God after our sin has separated us from him. Jesus brought restoration from exile (separation from God). He is forming a new, restored people from Jews and Gentiles, who form the numerous children. The Galatians – and we – can rejoice, for we are the children. We are the fulfillment. God truly is faithful to do more than we ask or imagine.

4. Galatians 4:28-31
a. How are the Galatians to view themselves?

- How are they children of promise? How would the reminder that they are children of promise lead them away from the false teaching of the Judaizers?
- What does verse 29 remind them about their identity?
- How are these reminders for you? How do they resonate with you?

Paul addresses his "brothers and sisters," meaning those in the Galatian churches who are sons and daughters of God the Father through faith in Jesus Christ. They are born by the power of the Spirit, like Isaac. They are the children of promise, meaning they, though Gentiles, are God's chosen people, the spiritual descendants of Isaac. Interestingly, the Judaizers, the biological descendants of Isaac, are spiritually of Ishmael. The Judaizers would hate this truthful analogy, which contradicts everything they believe about themselves and others.

b. How did the son born of the flesh (Ishmael) treat the son born by the power of the Spirit (Isaac)? In what way is it "the same now"?

- *Are there ways we see this today?*
- *How does Paul's quotation of Scripture in verse 30 relate to the Galatian issue?*
- *Why might it have been necessary to disassociate from the Judaizers?*
- *How does this relate to Galatians 3:17-18?*
- *What comfort can believers gain from Paul's words here? What good news is there for those who are seeking, but do not yet know Christ?*

Ishmael taunted and mocked Isaac (Genesis 21:8-10; if your group members object that is was not fair for Sarah to send Hagar and Ishmael away, acknowledge it is a complex argument and invite them to study *Discover Genesis,* and redirect attention to Galatians). Paul uses this episode to illustrate the situation between the Judaizers and the young Galatian Christians. The Galatian Christians may be perplexed as to why the Judaizers speak against their freedom in Christ if indeed Christ's sacrifice has fulfilled the law and set them free from its demands. Paul reassures them that this is to be expected, even as Ishmael, the son Abraham had received through his own efforts, taunted Isaac, the son born through faith in God's promise. That conflict will always be there, Paul assures his readers. Expect it.

Paul uses Scripture to reinforce his message. "Get rid of the slave woman and her son" – an echo of Sarah's plea to Abraham. The two do not belong together – salvation by faith in Christ has nothing to do with salvation through obedience to the law. No compromise is possible. This is not just a minor difference; this is false teaching and a different gospel (Galatians 1:9).

Paul's words are full of encouragement both to the Galatian believers and to believers today. Those who rely on the merits of Christ alone for salvation are sisters and brothers with Paul, children of the promise made to Abraham, and born by the power of the Spirit. They are heirs of an inheritance that those who live under the law can never receive.

They are members of a family that enjoys freedom, not slavery. Help your group discover these comforting assurances in this passage. Be sensitive to those who have not yet discovered the joy of being a son or daughter and watch for the Holy Spirit's working.

Discovering Our Stories

a. **What do we learn from Paul's pleas about loving others, persevering with others, and sharing truth?**

- *Who are you walking alongside of now? How are you showing love, truth, and persevering with them in their spiritual journey?*

b. **Paul spoke of knowing God, and being known by God and thus formed into Christlikeness. How are you growing in your knowledge of God and Christlikeness? How would you like to grow?**

c. **What is your next step as a result of this study?**

d. **Read Psalm 16 as an expression of devotion to the one, true living God, and as a song of joy for his fulfillment of his promises.**

More to Discover

Question 1a | Romans 6:6, 16-17 (slaves)

1b | John 13:18 (known by God)

2a | 1 Corinthians 11:1 ("become like me")
   1 Corinthians 9:19-23 ("became like you")

2b | Romans 4:6-9 (blessing)
   Ephesians 4:15 (telling the truth)
   Romans 12:11 (zeal)

2c | 1 Corinthians 4:15 (children)
   Romans 8:29; 2 Corinthians 3:18; Colossians 3:4 (Christ formed)
   Ephesians 4:13; Colossians 2:6-7 (evidence of Christ formed)

3b | Genesis 16:14; 21:1-13 (Hagar and Sarah)
  Hebrews 12:22; Revelation 21:2 (Jerusalem that is above)
  Romans 5:5, 8; 1 John 3:1; 4:8-10, 10 (God's love)
  John 8:33 (understanding of Paul's opponents)
3c | Isaiah 54:1 (barren woman)
4b | Genesis 21:8-10 (persecuted)

6 Galatians 5:1-15
Set Free in Christ

Optional Share Question

Do you like to run? Why or why not?

Running is one of the metaphors that Paul uses in this section. It captures some of the discipline and perseverance needed, as well as the obstacles (in this case, the Judaizers who are trying to trip them).

Some groups may not use the warm-up questions at all; but if there is a newcomer midway, or a visitor, these questions are often helpful to make all feel at ease again.

Getting Started

In chapter 5, Paul begins to shift his letter. He has shared his credentials, and explored truth, law, gospel, and salvation with the Galatians. He now begins to explore the implications for the Christian walk of the Galatians – and ours. The Galatians began their race well. How can they finish well? What does freedom look like in everyday life?

Additional Note for the Leader: Before you lead and discuss with group members, pray that the Holy Spirit will help them understand what Paul's words mean for their lives and for yours as well. Pray that the Holy Spirit, who empowers you to lead this lesson with wisdom and sensitivity, will also work in their hearts to help them understand and accept God's offer of a restored relationship, free from fear and guilt.

Discovering Together

1. Galatians 5:1

Glossary: yoke

a. **For what purpose does Christ set the believer free? What does this mean, in light of what we have studied so far in Galatians?**

- *What are we redeemed from in Galatians 3:13?*
- *What are they no longer under in Galatians 3:23-25?*
- *What were they slaves to in Galatians 4:3? in 4:9?*
- *What was the slave woman associated with in Galatians 4:24-25? What did Mount Sinai represent?*
- *What do you learn about God's desire for his people? What does this say about his character?*
- *Now that you have seen these all listed together, how would you like to respond to God?*

We are set free for freedom – Paul will spell this out further in this chapter. We are free from the law and its curse (Galatians 3:13, 23-25; 4:3-5). As per the law, commentator Philip Ryken comments:

> Christ has not set us free from the moral law, which is God's eternal will for his people, but from the law that leads to sin and death. This is the law that we break when we sin, that Satan uses to accuse us of our guilt, and that sentences us to death. But the gospel of free grace says that the law no longer has that kind of power over me.... [Jesus Christ] has freed me from the law's deadly curse against my sin. He has kept the law that I could not keep, paid the penalty I could not pay, and won the victory I could not win (p. 195).

We are free from sin and the devil (Hebrews 2:14-15; John 8:31-32, 34; Colossians 1:13-14). In short, Christian freedom means we are no longer under Satan's reign, controlled by sin, or under the curse of the law which leads to death. Rather, we are under Christ, under grace.

What are we free for? We are free for a life of faith, grace, and promise (Galatians 2:19-20; 3-4). We are free to run to the Father (Galatians 4:6-7). We are free for love and service (Galatians 5:6, 13-14). We are free for relationship with God and others, rather than for law and the pride and fear that can come with that.

Different cultures may have different conceptions of freedom, such as freedom from external restraints for radical self-independence. Christian freedom is not just freedom *from*, but freedom *for*. We are free to serve God (Romans 6:11-14).

You may use some of the following questions to explore you culture's idea:

- How does our culture define freedom? What images or words do people in our community use to describe it?
- How is Christian freedom different?
- What are we free to do?
- Do we still keep God's moral law? How does that show God's way to live by grace?
- How is the moral law different from a law that we have to keep in order to earn God's favor? What happens when we break this law? What does that lead to?

b. What caution does Paul give?

- Against whom are the believers to "stand firm"? What is the yoke that threatens to enslave them again?
- How does Matthew 11:28-30 differ? How does Jesus' yoke differ from the yoke of the law? Why do you think Jesus calls to weary people rather than to rested people? How do you see Jesus' compassion here, and in Galatians?

Paul charges his readers to resist the false teaching of the Judaizers. Some groups may want to discuss Jesus' offer to the Jews around him who were oppressed by the law's demands to rest and take his light yoke (Matthew 11:28-30). Jesus' offer of salvation is for those who are exhausted by trying to achieve salvation in their own strength.

---

2. Galatians 5:2-6

Glossary: circumcision, faith, grace, Holy Spirit, Jesus Christ, justification, law, righteousness

a. What obligation does circumcision require?

- Why might the Galatians feel that circumcision is important? What does it signify to them?

Circumcision means obligation to obey the whole law. Circumcision signifies entrance into the Jewish faith. All males who are born into the Jewish faith or who leave a pagan religion to become Jews are required to be circumcised.

b. Why might Christ be of no value to a person wanting to be circumcised?

- *Is the law able to deliver righteousness to those who try to gain their salvation by following it? Why not?*
- *For what does the believer eagerly await through the Holy Spirit? How does one receive this righteousness? Is it by good works or by faith?*
- *Is circumcision and keeping the law depending on self, or depending on Christ? How is it saying that the person thinks Christ's work is not sufficient?*
- *Is circumcision still the sign of covenant with God? How is Christ's blood the new sign? (Luke 22:19-20)*

Christ is of no value for those who want to earn their own salvation via acts like circumcision. For then the law would have to be kept in its entirety (which is impossible, as we have earlier discussed). We cannot depend on Christ *and* the law; it is either or. People are unable to achieve right standing with God by doing something in their own strength, such as obeying the law or undergoing circumcision. It cannot work that way because salvation does not depend on human effort. Righteousness is a gift of God which he gives freely to the person who believes in Jesus Christ. To reinforce Paul's teaching, you might read Romans 3:21-24 with your group.

If questions come up about circumcision, you may use questions like the following:

- *How does Deuteronomy 30:6 define circumcision?*
- *How does God's gift of righteousness through Christ make the rite of circumcision obsolete? What is the new righteousness based on in Romans 3:21-24?*

Believers no longer need to be circumcised. True circumcision in the Old Testament point to heart change (Deuteronomy 30:6), a symbol of cutting off sin. Jesus is our circumcision. He was cut off in death on the cross as he became sin for us. In other words, Jesus is our sign of the covenant. In him, we are included in God's people. Paul elaborates a bit in Colossians 2:9-13. If your group wonders, circumcision is not wrong – Paul reiterates in 1 Corinthians 7:17-20 that it is a secondary thing to obedience. Timothy was actually circumcised in order to help in his mission to the Jews (Acts 16:13).

Perhaps some group members may raise the question, does this mean a Christian can lose his or her salvation? If you think this is a question your group will raise, prepare questions beforehand. The Bible has some very explicit statements that true followers of Jesus cannot lose their salvation (such as John 6:37-40; 10:28-29). Furthermore, Paul does address them as brothers and sisters in the faith, as children of God and children of promise – these are notes of confidence (Galatians 3:26-27; 4:31; 5:10). God will ensure his true people persevere. However, these are real warnings that God will use to ensure they persevere. We can have assurance, in all our ups and downs of our spiritual journey, for Christ is enough. To choose legalism is to say that one no longer wants to be related to God through grace, but through self-effort, and self-effort will fall short. It shows a fundamental misunderstanding of God, his way, his grace, our sin and sinful human nature, and Christ's work. It is, in short, saying that Christ's death is not enough. Oh, let us exalt Christ for all he has done, all he is worthy of!

c. What does Paul say is "the only thing that counts"? Why does he say that?

- How is faith to express itself? How might believers today express their faith through love?
- What do you learn about what God desires?

Faith will show itself through love. Love comes as a result of faith, so it is ultimately the work of the Holy Spirit. Encourage members to suggest specific examples of faith expressing itself through love. Paul always taught that faith in Christ and a life of love must go hand in hand. As commentator William Barclay notes, "The essence of Christianity is not law but a personal relationship to Jesus Christ. The Christian's faith is founded not on a book but on a person; its dynamic is not obedience to any law but love to Jesus Christ." This will become clearer as you discuss verses 13-15.

3. Galatians 5:7-12

Glossary: cross of Christ

a. What does Paul say about those who are trying to mislead the Galatians? What indicates the intensity of his feelings?

- *How are the false teachers trying to "trip up" the Galatians?*
- *What happens when just a small amount of yeast is added to bread dough? How quickly does it grow? Does it affect just a small part of the dough, or the whole lump? How is this similar to the Judaizers' influence in the Galatian churches?*
- *What will they pay? Who will bring justice? What do we learn about God's defense of his people?*
- *What does Paul wish for them? How does this show the strength of Paul's feelings?*

The false teachers are trying to trip the Galatians. The yeast of their sin will contaminate them all. They are throwing others into confusion. They will pay the penalty, and Paul goes so far to say that he wishes they would emasculate themselves! Paul makes no effort to hide his anger at those who are leading his beloved Galatian believers away from the gospel.

One appropriate penalty, in Paul's judgment, is that these "agitators" cut away not only their foreskins but to castrate themselves as well. This is strong language, but Paul does not mean it as a coarse jest. Rather, he places the rite of circumcision on the same level with all the other pagan practices of the day, which the Galatians are undoubtedly aware of. Just as pagan priests cut themselves with knives in honor of their gods, hoping to gain favor, so Paul says circumcision as a means to salvation in the Christian church is simply an outmoded and ineffectual way to gain God's favor. It is no longer a sign of God's covenant with his people; its significance ended with the coming of Christ, who opened a new path to God – a path of faith.

b. What encouragement for the Galatian believers is in these verses?

- *How does Paul describe their "track record" in verse 7?*
- *Who was "the one who calls you"? How does this encourage you?*

- What confidence does Paul express (v. 10)? How can he be so confident? In whom is he confident? How might Philippians 1:6 and 2:12-13 express this as well?
- With what term does he still address the straying Galatians?
- What do we learn about the Lord in these verses as well?
- What encouragement do you find?

Paul compliments their earlier actions; they "were running a good race." If God calls them (present tense), Paul is affirming their belief. God can make them stand (Romans 14:4) and complete his good work in them (Philippians 1:6; 2:12-13). God's work is always the basis for Paul's confidence.

You may discuss Paul's attitude toward his readers. He makes every effort to mix tenderness and encouragement with his criticism and warnings:

- What is Paul's attitude toward his readers? How do you see a mix of encouragement and warning? What do you learn from this?
- In what ways does Paul serve as a model for Christians who must approach their erring brothers and sisters?

Paul does not question the Galatians' standing with God, but rather affirms them in genuine love. His criticism is meant to expose sin patterns.

c. What might Paul have meant by "the offense of the cross"?

- What do the Judaizers believe was necessary for their salvation? How does Christ's death on the cross do away with the Judaizers' system of righteousness? How does the cross become a stumbling block for them – something they resist and reject?
- Read the glossary note on "the cross of Christ." What is the view of crucifixion for the Romans, Greeks, and Jews? How does this help you understand how startling the cross may be? How could a crucified person be the way to righteousness? How could a Holy God be crucified?
- How does 1 Corinthians 1:18-25 help us understand how the cross may be a stumbling block of offense?
- How is the cross an offense today in our community?

- *What makes people want to earn their salvation on their own efforts, as the Judaizers try to do?*
- *How does this emphasize God's grace and love?*

For the Jews in general, the death of the Messiah is a definite stumbling block. It is unthinkable. How could God's anointed, his chosen one, be put to death? Also offensive is the fact that Christ's sacrificial death fulfilled the requirements of the law and forever broke down the wall between Jew and Gentile. In addition, it erased any mistaken belief that their own efforts could help them obtain righteousness. It is a blow to human pride. On some level, we want to at least partially deserve our salvation. This only emphasizes God's grace – there is nothing we could have done to save ourselves. But in his love and grace, he has completely done it all.

The cross still remains a point of confusion and objection to many Jews, Muslims, and others – to human pride. If desired, 1 Corinthians 1:18-25, also may help your group understand the offense of the cross.

You could also discuss Paul's persecution; this is also mentioned in the "Historical Snapshot."

- *How might the Judaizers and Jews persecute Paul for not preaching circumcision?*
- *Do you recall any of these events from Acts? How might the Galatians remember that? (Possibly Acts 13:35, 50; 14:1-2, 5, 19)*

All of Paul's missionary journeys ae characterized by persecution from angry Jews who realize that the good news of the gospel undermines their whole system of laws and rituals. If he instead would preach that circumcision is necessary for salvation, then they would have no reason to differ with him. He would agree with their basic belief: that obedience to the law is essential to be right with God.

4. Galatians 5:13-15
Glossary: flesh

a. How does Paul suggest freedom might be misused? How is it to be used?

- *What are some examples of indulging the flesh?*
- *If we do not have the law, does that mean we can live however we want?*

- *Why might we be tempted to use our freedom wrong?*
- *What are ways you have seen this freedom used right? What helps us keep this perspective, that we are free to love?*

Freedom is to love. Paul may be answering another criticism of the Judaizers. Evidently many Jewish Christians fear that his message of liberty from the law means that believers can engage in immoral or offensive things in the name of Christian freedom. Paul assures his readers that freedom in Christ does not mean the liberty to do anything one desires. Paul does not object to the law as a guide to living a holy life; he faults the law only as a means of obtaining salvation.

b. How is the law summed up?

- *What is to be the believer's motive for obeying the law?*
- *How does Matthew 22:37-40 point to the purpose of the law?*
- *If you look at the Ten Commandments, how might they all be fulfilled in love? (Exodus 20:1-17)*
- *What might the law still show us about God's character? What might we learn, for instance, about God's character from the Ten Commandments?*
- *How does Jesus' fulfillment of the law change our relationship to the law?*
- *How does Paul see it as a guide for Christian living in this passage?*
- *What is the difference between using the law as a way to earn salvation, versus seeing it as a guide for how to live by God's power?*

Paul introduces a rather startling paradox in these verses. The law is not a way to salvation or justification, but Christians are to fulfill it – by love (Leviticus 19:18).

First, there is a new perspective on the law that understands its essence. Paul makes his thoughts even clearer, perhaps, in Romans 13:8-10. The Old Testament prophets and Jesus were always pointing Jews back to the essence of the law (for a few instances, Micah 6:6-8; Matthew 9:13; 22:37-40).

Second, there is a new relationship to the law. The old relationship of *doing* the law for salvation is done. Since Jesus has fulfilled the law for us, we are no longer debtors to the law. It can no longer hold us in custody of our sin, and lead to death. Through Jesus we can approach the law from a place of salvation. Now the law serves us as a guide as we are called, in our freedom, to serve the Lord in love. It still shows us God's character, and his will. God's character, and thus his basic moral ways for us to live, has not changed (for example, the Ten Commandments, Exodus 20:1-17). As Charles Spurgeon says:

> What is God's law now? Is it not above a Christian – it is under a Christian. Some men hold God's law like a rod, in terror, over Christians, and say, "If you sin, you will be punished with it." It is not so. The law is under a Christian; it is for him to walk on, to be his guide, his rule, his pattern: "we are not under the law, but under grace." Law is the road which guides us, not the rod which drives us, nor the spirit which actuates us. The law is good and excellent, if it keep its place. (cited by Ryken, p. 223)

Third, there is a new power. As we will discover in the next section, we have a new heart and the very Spirit of God himself to help us live in love, and thus fulfill the law.

c. What caution does Paul give in verse 15? Why do you think he does so at this point?

- *Why might loving one's neighbor be difficult? How does this seem to be showing up in the Galatian church?*
- *Imagine yourself in the Galatian church. What might biting and devouring each other look like?*
- *What is the result of biting and devouring each other?*
- *How have you seen the lack of love destroying one another? How have you seen love building unity and giving life to one another?*

Immediately after the call to love one another, Paul shows one manifestation of the lack of love, and its result. If the Galatians keep fighting and attacking each other (Paul uses vivid animal imagery with the words "biting" and "devouring"), they will destroy the church. In contrast, love will build each other up. Paul also introduces the idea of the sinful nature in this passage, something he will explore further in verses 16-26.

Discovering Our Stories

a. What is the freedom for which Christ has set the believer free? How does this freedom find expression in the Christian's life?

Help your group review. They may name several benefits. Christ brings freedom from God's anger, the power of sin, a guilty conscience, fear of death, and so on. This new freedom brings with it a life of power in the Spirit, a new and healthy self-esteem, the ability to receive and give God's love, and a desire for joyful obedience.

b. **What does it look like to fulfill the law of love? What is one way God is empowering you or calling you to do that in your life right now, or within your faith community?**

c. **What is your next step as a result of this study?**

d. **Read Psalm 25:1-15 as a psalm of hope (Galatians 5:5) and of guidance.**

More to Discover

Question 1a | John 8:31-32, 34; Romans 6:11-14; Colossians 1:13-14; Hebrews 2:14-15 (free)

1b | Matthew 11:28-30 (yoke)

2b | Luke 22:19-20 (sign of the covenant)

Romans 3:21-24 (gaining righteousness)

Deuteronomy 30:6; Acts 16:13; 1 Corinthians 7:17-20; Colossians 2:9-13 (circumcision)

John 6:37-40; 10:28-29 (security in Christ)

3b | Romans 14:4; Philippians 1:6; 2:12-13 (Paul's confidence)

3c | 1 Corinthians 1:18-25 (offense of the cross)

Acts 13:35, 50; 14:1-2, 5, 19 (persecuted)

4b | Leviticus 19:18; Exodus 20:1-17; Micah 6:6-8; Matthew 9:13; 22:37-40; Romans 13:8-10 (fulfillment of the law)

7 Galatians 5:16-6:10
Life in the Spirit

Optional Share Question

Which way best communicates love to you? Words of affirmation, quality time, physical touch, acts of service, or a gift?

Whether Dr. Gary Chapman's theory of five love languages is correct or not, it is a great introduction to this lesson which speaks of love and doing good to one another. If you use this optional share question, you may write down which love languages your group members have.

Getting Started

Paul said previously that to love was to fulfill the law. He hinted, however, that this life faced opposition. This opposition will be brought to light in this lesson. Yet, at the core of this lesson is the question of how believers are to fulfill the command "Love your neighbor as yourself." Is it just another bondage, a struggle in one's own strength to please and obey God? Today we will see the provision God has made for our lives.

Additional Note to the Leader: Pray that the fruit of the Spirit will be evident in your own life to witness to the truth of this passage and reveal the Holy Spirit's presence in your life. Pray that your group members who have not made Christ Lord and Savior may be irresistibly drawn to him through the liberating message Paul brings.

Discovering Together

1. Galatians 5:16-18

Glossary: flesh, Holy Spirit, law

a. Why does Paul encourage the Galatians to live by the Holy Spirit? What might it mean to live by the Holy Spirit?

- *Who is the Holy Spirit?*
- *What does the image of "walking" convey?*
- *What will we not do in verse 16?*
- *If we are not under the law (v. 18), how does God help us live a pleasing life? What does this say about God's character? How much is he willing to help us?*
- *What do we learn about ourselves? Who do we have with us? How does this show how we cannot do the Christian life by the flesh, by our own efforts?*

We need the Holy Spirit because his presence within us is a sign that we are heirs of the promise Abraham received. While believers still struggle with their sinful natures, living by the Spirit means they are empowered by the Spirit to live for God; his strength is shaping their mind, heart, and actions. Make sure your group understands who the Holy Spirit is – in various cultures, there are many other spirits. Paul has already said that the Galatians began by the Holy Spirit, and are promised the Spirit (Galatians 3:3, 14; 5:5). The glossary has further references to help understand the Spirit. God is so committed to forming a holy people, to us, that we have the very Spirit of God, God himself, helping us to live a life pleasing to God!

b. What does the sinful nature desire? What does the Holy Spirit desire? What is the result of the conflict?

- *Why do the flesh and the Spirit conflict with each other?*
- *Does this battle take place in the outer world or within the inner self?*
- *Is it possible not to choose sides in this conflict?*

We are entering a battleground in this passage, a direct conflict between two opposing forces. As Paul describes this battle, it should become clear that it takes place within us, not outside of us – although outside circumstances can create the context. It is the struggle between fallen, sinful human nature and a godly, Christ-reflecting life in the Spirit. We cannot serve both the flesh and God.

You may choose to ask follow up questions exploring the Holy Spirit's leading in our lives:

- *How does such a life require a close dependence on God?*
- *What does it mean to be led by the Holy Spirit? What is the Holy Spirit's role? What is our role?*
- *Does this mean we do not do anything? (Philippians 2:12-13; Ephesians 4:22-24)*
- *How does this passage encourage you? How does it encourage you that God remains intimately involved to empower you to live a pleasing life?*

As Christians are born again in Christ through the Holy Spirit's power, not by their own efforts, so they are also to live godly lives through the Holy Spirit's power, not their own. Romans 7:18-19, 22-25 shows how powerless we are in our sinful human nature, but deliverance is in Christ. Romans 8:1-11 shows the victory we can have as we walk by the Spirit.

Be aware that verse 17 will vary in different translations (even the 1984 NIV is different from the 2011 NIV). Our flesh is actively warring, but the Spirit is triumphantly on our side.

Even though we have the Holy Spirit, we still struggle. You may wish to explore this.

- *Do believers struggle with the desire to sin?*
- *Is there hope for the person who truly wishes to put off the deeds of the sinful nature? Does Paul suggest that this can be done in one's own strength? (Romans 7:18-19, 22-25; 8:3)*
- *What is the Holy Spirit's role in the struggle described in verses 16-18? What does this tell us about living by the Holy Spirit?*

Encourage your group to mention some specific examples that help illustrate this struggle between the sinful nature and the Spirit's desires. You might think of some examples from your own life to help them get started. Be honest and authentic here. Let them know Christians still struggle with sin and experience the pain of living in a fallen world (1 Corinthians 10:13). Be careful, however, not to force responses. Pray for sensitivity in the Spirit.

2. Galatians 5:19-21

Glossary: debauchery, idolatry, impurity, kingdom of God, orgies, sexual immorality

a. What do these verses teach about sinful human nature, that is, the flesh?

- Why might Paul include envy, jealousy, dissensions and selfish ambition? How might all people be included?
- What might idolatry look like in our culture? (see glossary)
- How is this truth reflected in the news we hear or read daily?
- What happens to these sins when we confess them? What is God willing to do for all of these sins?

Paul does not paint a beautiful portrait of the sinful human soul. Within each of us, he says, lies the potential to indulge in immoral and unlawful acts. His list demonstrates a range of sins, too, demonstrating that all sins are serious in God's eyes. Some of your group members may think of the sins Paul lists as things that they have not done. Others may be living with the painful – and probably hidden – reality of what Paul is saying. Gently lead them to see that Paul is saying everyone used to live to gratify the flesh (Ephesians 2:1-5). This was all of us.

Though we might not bow down to idols of wood or stone, do we ever give our primary love and allegiance to something other than God? The seeds of the sinful nature lie in all of us; that is what prevents anyone from living a perfect life under the law. Again, be sensitive to those in your group who may outwardly appear to be quite secure, but inwardly are dealing with agonizing situations that cause great pain. Pray that you may radiate the love and acceptance of Christ to them.

Ensure that all know that forgiveness and cleansing is available for every sin. No matter what is done in the past, Christ's death and his perfect life can cover and cleanse (1 John 1:9; Hebrews 10:22; Psalm 103:10-12). As Paul says in verse 24, we are crucified. We are new creations (2 Corinthians 5:17). We have the Spirit to help us. Paul's words of warning are to those who habitually walk in the flesh.

b. Why does Paul warn against these things so strongly?

- How might our habitual walk show whether we live by the flesh or by the Holy Spirit? What kind of life or person might Paul be referring to here? Does Paul mean that a believer who falls into any of these sins will be barred from the kingdom of God? Or is he referring to those who give their lives over completely to the natural desires of the sinful nature?

- Why would it be impossible for those who live completely by the sinful nature to inherit this kingdom? What do their lives reveal about their relationship with God as Father?
- Where have we seen the talk of inheritance before? (Galatians 3:18, 29; 4:7) Who is an heir?
- What is the kingdom of God? Why is that an inheritance? How is it a gift? How did we become heirs?

Paul warns that if a person lives like this – in other words, they give themselves over completely to the natural desires of the sinful nature – they will not inherit the kingdom of God. The Greek uses the participle, emphasizing the habitual walk. They clearly show they have no interest in God or serving God. They are condemning themselves by their actions and their choice to reject God and his ways. The consequence is not for their behavior alone, but for their rejection of God.

Paul has spoken of being heirs before. Those who believe are children of God for whom an inheritance is promised (Galatians 4:7). For those members of your group who do not know Christ yet, this is an invitation. Paul here refers to it as the kingdom of God. It is appropriate to call it an inheritance, as we receive it by adoption, by grace (Galatians 4:5-7). It is a gift. Romans 14:17 describes the kingdom as "righteousness, peace, and joy in the Holy Spirit." The glossary will also have additional references.

3. Galatians 5:22-26
Glossary: cross of Christ

a. Why does Paul call these characteristics "fruit"? Why should those who belong to Christ bear this fruit in their lives?

- Do you think the Galatians might struggle with some of these sins still? What does Paul think is possible for them?
- Whose fruit is this? Whose power will produce the godliness and holiness that the law teaches?

- How does a tree produce fruit? How might Luke 6:43-45 help us understand this as well?
- How is the fruit connected to being led by the Spirit? (vv. 16-18)
- What do we learn about the character of God and the Holy Spirit that this is what he will produce?
- What do you learn about the work of the Holy Spirit?
- What should we do to grow the fruit of the Holy Spirit in us?
- How do these virtues spring from love for God and others? How are they related to each other?
- What would our lives be like if we lived consistently with this fruit? How would our relationships be different? Our community?
- How does this fulfill the law? (Galatians 5:14)
- What makes it difficult to show this fruit in our lives? How does it encourage you that God himself works in you to produce these?

The Galatians are likely struggling with many of the sins in verses 19-21, yet Paul says that they can walk by the Spirit and have this fruit. Realizing this may encourage your group.

S. J. Mikolaski writes that "fruit is a collective noun designating crop, or harvest, and suggests the many-sided character of a virtuous life." Explore this metaphor with your group. Fruit is something that is produced. It comes from the Spirit's seeds in our life, just as a tree naturally produces its own fruit. Help your group see that the image of fruit is directly connected with Paul's teaching on the Spirit-led life (vv. 16-18). We see God's own nature in this fruit – he is loving, joyful, peace-making, etc. The Spirit produces the fruit, but we must remain in Christ, love him, remember him, and seek to follow him. Fruit metaphors are used elsewhere: Ephesians 5:9; Philippians 1:11; Luke 6:43-45. In John 15:5, the fruit of the Spirit is connected to Jesus' life in us. These might be said to be facets of one fruit, for they are all interrelated. Most importantly, these will truly fulfill the law (Galatians 5:14).

Be careful not to make this merely an intellectual discussion. Acknowledge that we do not always show this fruit in our lives. Ask which aspect of the fruit is most difficult for them. Share your own struggles. Emphasize that it is only God working in our lives that enables us to display these Spirit-filled qualities.

To begin transitioning to the following question, you may compare with your group the fruit of the Spirit with the acts of the sinful nature. Rather than doing this with individual qualities, however, ask your group to identify the basic attitudes that underlie these two ways of life. You may write questions similar to the following for your group:

- *Who are people who live by their sinful nature trying to please and serve? Are God's wishes important to them? Are they concerned with the needs and wishes of others?*
- *Who do people who live by the Spirit seek to please and serve? Is the self the center of their universe?*
- *Look again at verses 16-18 and the battle. How do verses 19-22 show this conflict?*

b. What might it mean to "crucify the sinful nature"? How is that possible?

- *How is this related to our conversation about Galatians 2:19-20?*
- *How completely must the believer leave behind his or her allegiance to the sinful nature? In what sense have Christians "died" to their old passions and desires?*
- *Does that mean that they no longer have sinful desires?*

Paul's use of *crucify* shows the force of the totality of change and its connection with the death of Christ. This section reaffirms Paul's statement in 2:20. In Romans 6:11-14 Paul offers additional words of instruction concerning crucifying the sinful nature. You may want to read that passage with your group, too. Believers are "dead" to their sinful flesh; it no longer has power over them. Believers are still tempted, but they now have power to follow the Spirit and live for God because the Holy Spirit is within them and empowers them.

c. What might it mean to keep in step with the Holy Spirit?

- *What does it suggest about the one who is setting the direction for a person's life?*
- *How might a believer get out of step with the Holy Spirit? Why would this be bad for a believer?*
- *What example from your life can you give of keeping in step with the Holy Spirit?*

- *What is Paul's warning? Why might he have given it at this point (see also v. 15)?*
- *How might this have applied to the Galatian congregations?*

Perhaps continuing with a military image of conflict, we are to march in rhythm with the Spirit. We need to submit every aspect of our lives to God, who sets the direction for our lives. Here we see both our role and God's role: we are given the Spirit and his power and his fruit, but we are called to walk and to keep in step with the Spirit. We are saved, so let us live like it!

Paul warns especially against the sins of conceit, envy, and provoking each other. Perhaps, having proven that the Judaizers were wrong, Paul may be concerned that those who have not fallen for their heresy will become conceited, provoking and insulting those who have fallen, and will allow envy and strife to set in.

4. Galatians 6:1

Glossary: sin

How is sin to be dealt with in the Christian community?

- *What is the goal of such action?*
- *What does it mean to restore?*
- *Why is gentleness an important part of the restoration process?*
- *What do you see of God's heart in his desire for a sinner to be restored? For others to treat them gently?*
- *What might be the opposite of restoring? What other attitudes might people have toward someone who sins, or is shown to be in the wrong?*
- *How might this apply to the situation in Galatia?*
- *Have you had to personally speak with someone about an uncomfortable situation? How did you approach the situation and what was the outcome? Or has someone had to help you?*

Paul says that those who are filled with the Spirit (spiritual) should gently help to restore the sinner. The word *restore* implies healing, bringing something back to its original health or condition. Again, be aware that group members may be dealing with sin and brokenness on a very personal level. Let them see Christ's forgiveness and compassion through your love and acceptance. You may also read John 8:1-11 for an instance of Jesus' acknowledgement that we are all sinners and his forgiveness and restoration.

Paul warns against the innate desire in every human to be on the "right" side of an issue. In their zeal to be right, people may often criticize mercilessly in an attitude of self-righteousness. Here Paul again implies that believers may be "caught in a sin" at one time or another. Indeed, he warns those who have not fallen that they may well be tempted at some other time.

5. Galatians 6:2-6

Glossary: burden

> **What is the Galatians' responsibility to each other? To themselves?**

- *The Galatians have been eager to follow the law. What does Paul urge them to do instead?*
- *How does verse 2 relate to John 13:34?*
- *What might burdens be? What are practical ways we can carry each other's burdens today?*

Love, expressed in carrying each other's burdens, is shown again to be the fulfillment of the law and of Christ's command in John 13:34. These burdens might be physical, material, spiritual, or financial.

To explore their responsibility to themselves, you could consider questions such as the following:

- *How might living under the law lead a person to "think he is something when he is nothing"? How might it emphasize self-effort?*
- *Why might this be deceiving oneself? Are they able to keep the law? Would keeping the law to the best of their ability gain what they desired?*
- *Why should a person test his or her own actions? What does it mean to test? What might they test them for? What are they to test against? How might believers test against God's standard rather than others?*
- *How does the salvation by grace make it unnecessary to compare one's works with those of others? What is the opposite of comparing*

ourselves? What would a life that rested completely in Christ look like? How can we get there?

- Why are we tempted to compare ourselves to one another? How is the ability to rest in grace, rather than compare, counter-cultural?
- In what sense can believers take pride in themselves?
- What responsibility does Paul place on those who "receive instruction in the word"?

Paul cautions the Galatians on being prideful. Looking at verse 3, the Judaizers' insistence on obeying the law put the emphasis on the self: "I am able to achieve salvation in my own strength." Yet, human effort is not able to achieve true fruit of the Spirit.

Verses 4 and 5 deal with believers' responsibility for their own actions. Believers are to examine their works (1 Corinthians 13:5-6). Are we keeping in step with the Spirit? (Galatians 5:16) Are we loving our neighbor? (Galatians 5:14) Are we carrying the burden for others? (Galatians 6:2) Are we living a life of love by the Spirit and with his strength, not ours? We are to test our works against God's standards, not compare ourselves to one another. This can be counter-cultural for many of us; many cultures encourage that competition. We are called to rest in grace; Christ is our reputation and righteousness. We do not rest on our own reputation. Yet, since salvation is by grace and our fruit is by the Spirit, we have no basis to judge or compare. Everything that is given to us is a gift by God himself.

Scholars admit that it is difficult to connect verse 6 with Paul's train of thought, both in the preceding and the following verses. However, his command is clear: Give your spiritual teachers not only your affection and attention but also your financial support. Paul is well acquainted with this need (Philippians 4:10-19). Paul recognizes the Christian life is a life of sharing in the needs, burdens, joys, and sorrows of other believers.

---

6. Galatians 6:7-10

a. What does verse 7 teach us about God, especially in light of the verses that follow?

- Is anyone able to hide anything from God? Who judges our lives?
- What kind of harvest does God want for us?
- What determines our "harvest"?

God, who searches the hearts of all people, is easily able to discern the motivations which guide the choices we make in life (see Jeremiah 17:10; Psalm 139:23-24). He knows whether we are living for his glory or for our own. Some in your group may view God as a harsh judge. Be aware, and perhaps help them reframe. What if God is one who delights in us and invites us to share in his happiness? (Matthew 25:21) Who makes our efforts grow? (1 Corinthians 3:6) Who ensures what we sow is not in vain, but fruitful? (John 15:2, 5; 1 Corinthians 15:58) Who gives praise? (Romans 2:29; 1 Corinthians 4:5)

b. What does Paul mean by "sowing" and "reaping"?

- *What are the two ways we can sow?*
- *Can the "acts of the sinful nature" – hatred, immorality, rage, selfish ambition, and so on – lead to anything but destruction?*
- *How does the fruit of the Holy Spirit foster and nurture life? How does this fruit in a person's life give evidence that that person has received eternal life through Christ?*
- *Is it possible to plant dandelion seeds and get roses instead? What determines the harvest of one's life?*
- *What kind of harvest do you want?*
- *How is each new day a new opportunity to plant new seeds?*

Paul turns again to the struggle between the old nature and the life of the Holy Spirit.

People who "sow to the Spirit" are in the Holy Spirit and thus, even though they may struggle, they also begin to produce the fruit Paul mentioned earlier. Be careful not to discourage those who are struggling with sin. Paul's attitude is not judgmental or condemning. Let group members know that no one is beyond the grace of God. But while there is forgiveness for sin, believers still must deal with the consequences of sin.

- *How does Paul encourage the Galatians in verse 9? What are temptations to become weary in doing good? What is the promise as we persevere?*
- *How are we to treat others in verse 10? Give concrete examples, if possible.*

Discovering Our Stories

a. What are some specific ways that life in the Holy Spirit is to be practiced within the Christian fellowship? In daily life?

- *What is the Holy Spirit impressing on your heart? Is there a step he is calling you to take?*
- *How does life in the Holy Spirit call us to help one another? Is there someone or something he is placing on your heart?*

b. How does this lesson encourage you to persevere in doing good?

- *What is God calling you to persevere in right now? What is challenging for you? How can we as a group help you?*

c. What is your next step as a result of this study?

d. Read Psalm 139 as a prayer to the God who knows our days, our gifts, our works, and what we sow – and uses such knowledge in love and comes to our defense.

More to Discover

Question 1b | Romans 7:18-19, 22-25; 8:1-11; 1 Corinthians 10:13; Ephesians 4:22-24; Philippians 2:12-13 (flesh and Spirit)

2a | Ephesians 2:1-5 (gratify the flesh)
 Psalm 103:10-12; Hebrews 10:22; 1 John 1:9 (forgiveness)
 2 Corinthians 5:14-17 (new life and power)

2b | Romans 14:17 (kingdom of God)

3a | Luke 6:43-45; John 15:5; Ephesians 5:9; Philippians 1:11 (fruit)

3b | Romans 6:11-14 (crucified the flesh)

4 | John 8:1-11 (gently restore)

5 | John 13:34 (law of Christ)
 1 Corinthians 13:5-6 (test their own actions)
 Philippians 4:10-19 (share with instructor)

6a | Psalm 139:23-24; Jeremiah 17:10 (God cannot be mocked)
 Matthew 25:21; John 15:2, 5; Romans 2:29; 1 Corinthians 3:6; 4:5; 15:58 (sowing and reaping)

8 Galatians 6:11-18
A Brief Benediction

Optional Share Question

If you could boast about something you have done what would it be?

Getting Started

Paul concludes with a boast – but a boast that turns things upside down. With a final contrast, he will compare the boasting of the false teachers, and his own boasting. What is really important to boast in? We will see many of the themes of the letter in this small chapter, which gives an excellent opportunity to weave them all together.

Additional Note to the Leader:
Commentator Charles Erdman suggests that Paul's closing statements echo the three main divisions in his letter, though in reverse order: verses 11-13 rebuke the Judaizers and expose their selfish motives and deception; verses 14-16 emphasize the importance of justification by faith; and verse 17 restates Paul's authority as an apostle of Christ. At the end of this lesson review these basic themes and answer any questions your group may have on Paul's defense of freedom in Christ.

Discovering Together

1. Galatians 6:11-13

Glossary: circumcision, cross of Christ, flesh, Judaizers, law

What are the motives of the false teachers in the Galatian churches and why?

- *How do they want to appear in front of people?*
- *Why might their teachings help them avoid persecution? From whom?*
- *With whose welfare are they concerned?*

- How are they trying to do it? What does "means of the flesh" mean?
- How might some Christians want to make a good impression outward for their own reputation?
- How much do the interests of the world matter to you? What effect do they have on the internal condition of your heart?

Paul becomes very blunt here; he states openly that his opponents' main concern is to make a good outward impression. Rather than defending and teaching the true gospel, they twist it to avoid persecution at the hands of the Jews. You may refer back to the discussion at Galatians 5:11. They are chiefly concerned about their welfare, and their ability to boast.

The Judaizers want to make Christianity more acceptable to their Jewish brothers by saying, "Christianity is not a radical change from the Jewish religion. See, we even circumcise the believing Gentiles according to the laws of Moses. Is not that a sign of our intent to completely obey the Jewish ceremonial regulations and to base our faith on that system of laws?" The Judaizers hope that this will make Christianity more acceptable to the Jewish community. Yet it is at the cost of the true gospel.

To continue to the following question, you may want to discuss how Paul reveals the burden they place on others, so that they can boast:

- How are they placing a burden on the Gentiles? Can they carry that burden?
- Can anyone keep the law perfectly? (James 2:10).

What hypocrites! exclaims Paul. They know very well that even the circumcised Jews can not keep the law perfectly; yet they insist that circumcision is necessary for Gentile Christians, bringing them under the obligations of the law again.

Study Note: It was Paul's custom to dictate his letters to a scribe and then write the closing words in his own hand to verify that he was the author. This was a common custom in the ancient world. The large letters he refers to may indicate poor eyesight, or they may be his way of drawing emphasis to his conclusion.

2. Galatians 6:14-16

Glossary: Israel, peace

a. How does Paul's boasting contrast with the Judaizers' boasting?

- *What does Paul boast in? And the Judaizers?*
- *Whom does Paul seek to please first and foremost? Whom do the Judaizers seek to please?*
- *What is Paul's concern for the Galatians? The Judaizers' concern?*
- *Where does Paul find his glory and his identity? What about the Judaizers?*
- *Does Paul seek to avoid persecution? What about the Judaizers?*
- *How much importance does Paul place on external acts? The law? What about the Judaizers?*
- *How do you picture the expression on Paul's face? What do you imagine his emotions to be like as he writes this?*

You may want to encourage your group to complete a chart, with Judaizers on one side, and Paul's teaching on the other. This may be helpful for some in your group. A few additional verses are given; only use these if they are helpful.

A variety of themes are woven together here – above all showing Paul's deep grasp and awe of what Christ has done. Paul boasts in the cross alone, to please God (Galatians 1:10). He is deeply concerned for the Galatians (v. 13; Galatians 4:19). Paul finds his identity and his glory in the cross (v. 14; 2:19-20). He is not afraid of persecution (5:11). He recognizes here that neither circumcision nor uncircumcision mean anything; they are empty acts. What counts is the new birth, internal transformation that reveals itself in a new person walking with the Spirit to love others. Circumcision shows a fundamental misunderstanding of the new birth – as if circumcision and law-keeping somehow complete that (Galatians 3:3). Reliance on circumcision is what the Judaizers boast in.

b. What happens through the cross of Christ? Explain.

- *How is it possible to boast in the cross, a symbol of shame and criminal punishment?*
- *What name does Paul link with the cross? Why is it important it is Christ's cross, and not just any other? How is his death unique?*

- *How has Christ made it a symbol of victory and new life?*
- *In what way does the cross symbolize the basic nature of Christianity?*

Christ takes on sin's curse for us. This is how we become a new creation. This is the only way we can boast.

Explore first the basic understanding of the cross. The glossary may help your group grasp the paradox of trying to boast in the cross.

Commentator S. J. Mikolaski notes that "by using Christ's full title Paul intends to reaffirm not only the indispensable redemptive act, but the divine nature of Christ. . . . The cross is God's cross, therefore God's way, therefore the only way of salvation."

You may also examine Paul's meaning of "world."

- *What does it mean to die to something? If you died to something, do you think it would exert control over you?*
- *Does the "world" literally mean the physical environment in which we live? What had Paul died to in Galatians 2:19? How does Galatians 4:3 help us understand what Paul means by world? How might it be in contrast to the new creation Paul mentions in v. 15?*
- *How are Christians called to be crucified to the world, and to act as though the world has been crucified to them?*
- *What does dying allow us to live for? How does it lead to the new creation?*

Dying to something means it no longer controls you. The "world" likely refers to the entire old order – including the law (Galatians 2:19), the elemental forces that kept people in slavery (Galatians 4:3). It is the sway of influences of the sinful order outside of Jesus. So, too, we are called to be set apart from the systems of injustice, power, oppression, the law, self-righteousness, selfish ambitions, the grasp of other religious powers, etc. We are free to live solely for Christ. By his death, he has removed the curse of the law, and we can rejoice in that freedom.

c. What does Paul say really counts in the Christian life? How does this relate to the Galatian controversy?

- *How are circumcision and uncircumcision nothing? How might Paul have died to those?*
- *What does Paul mean by "new creation"?*

- *How do people become new creations when they are crucified to the world and the world to them?*
- *Compare 5:6 and 6:15. What counts? How are these related?*
- *How does this concept of new creation fit in with Paul's words in Galatians 5:16-25?*
- *What do we learn about God and his desire and plan when he makes us new creations?*

Paul elaborates on one aspect of the world that he has died to – circumcision or uncircumcision. Dead to it, these external acts hold no sway over him (or the Galatians, or us) and thus count for nothing.

"New creation" refers to the new life which God brings to the individual human heart to express itself in love. A new life to love God and others is what really counts. The cross of Christ offers a "fresh start" to any person who believes (2 Corinthians 5:17). We are just the firstfruits, signs of an entirely new creation (Revelation 21:4-5). We experience in part what Christ will make true when he comes again for the entire world. We see God's heart to restore, his heart to re-create according to his goodness, his faithfulness to his creation and his plan, and his power to make all things new.

d. How does being a new creation bring us hope?

- *How are we not only given a fresh start, but a new power?*
- *How can the power of the past be broken? How does our past – no matter how dark or how good – no longer define us?*

As new creations, there is hope, no matter how dark one's past. We have more than a fresh start – we are not just given a blank slate to try again in our own strength. Indeed, we are given a new power by the Spirit, a new heart to love God and others.

e. What comes to those who follow the true teaching of the gospel (v. 16)?

- *Who or what was Israel in the Old Testament? How is Paul using this for the Galatians? How do the Galatians show themselves to be the true people of God through faith? (Galatians 3:7, 28-29; 4:26, 31)*
- *What does Paul mean by peace and mercy? Why are these words especially appropriate here?*
- *How had the Galatians turned away from mercy?*

Paul gives his readers a benediction as part of his closing comments. Paul refers to both believing Jew and believing Gentile as "Israel of God." Galatians 3:7, 28-29; 4:26, 31; Philippians 3:3 are additional verses that will help your group make this connection.

Paul desires God's peace and mercy for those who live by the teaching of the true gospel. Focus especially on mercy – God's undeserved love and favor in Christ. Be aware that Paul's strong emphasis on salvation by grace may be a new message to some who have grown up with a strong emphasis on self-achievement, or other religious influences. Salvation by grace alone is not easy to accept; we instinctively say, "But isn't there anything I have to do?" We want to be in control of our lives. It is difficult to understand that freedom can come only when we surrender control to God. Pray that your group members will be able to understand and receive this message of God's grace, offered freely apart from our own efforts.

3. Galatians 6:17-18

Glossary: grace, mercy

a. What does Paul point to as a sign of his authority?

- *How did he open his letter? Why might he close with an emphasis on authority again?*
- *How do all of his scars from persecution show his authority? What does it say about the level of commitment to the truth he proclaimed to the Galatians?*
- *What request does he make?*
- *In what way do Paul's "marks" prove that he is a soldier for Jesus, a slave to Christ, and a devotee of the Christian religion?*
- *Why might these marks be especially relevant in a case where the Judaizers are emphasizing a physical mark, circumcision?*

Paul has suffered much for the gospel (2 Corinthians 11:24-25). Perhaps some of the Galatians remember his stoning (Acts 14:19). Paul regards his scars as proof that he has been faithful to the gospel of Jesus, for only on account of his faithfulness to that gospel has he received his scars. Paul wishes to be rid of the harassment of the Judaizers, who are constantly looking for an outward sign. Paul shows them a sign – the marks and scars on his body which he suffered for the sake of Christ.

If desired, you could elaborate on the study note. Paul's marks show how he has fought for Jesus, served Jesus, and knew the fellowship of his sufferings.

As a review question, you could ask:

- What does this book tell us about Paul's relationship to Christ?

Study Note: The scars on Paul's body testify to the beatings and physical abuse he had suffered as a result of his faithfulness to the gospel of Jesus. In Paul's culture three classes of people received the "marks" – scars or ritual cuttings – that Paul refers to: slaves, soldiers, and followers of certain religions.

b. How does Paul close the letter? How would you put this in your own words?

- Why do you think Paul concludes his letter with an emphasis on grace?
- What would it be like to feel the grace of the Lord Jesus Christ with you?
- How does he address his readers? How does this reflect his faith in God's work in them?
- What thoughts are left uppermost in their minds?

Though Paul ends his letter quite abruptly, his tone is still warm. Paul's concluding benediction, though brief, is nonetheless rich. Paul emphasizes grace. Review the glossary definition if you think anyone is unclear of its meaning. Encourage your members to explain this in their own words. Not only will this bring the meaning of the term closer to their own experience, but it will help you sense how well they have understood Paul's message in Galatians.

4. Review of Galatians 1-6

a. Summarize the marks of the true gospel (1:11-12; 2:20; 3:14, 22, 27-28; 4:6; 5:24) and of the false teaching of the Judaizers (2:21; 3:12; 4:3, 10; 5:4).

b. Paul speaks here of a new creation, which is related to his discussion of the new life in Christ in chapters 2-4. How does one receive this new life? What does Paul reject as a way to gain this salvation?

c. Paul has focused in chapters 4-6 on one thing that Christ has secured for us in the cross, freedom. Practically speaking, what does this freedom involve? How does it change one's life?

- *Has Paul presented a convincing argument? Why or why not?*
- *What is the place of the law in the Christian life?*

d. How do Paul's arguments seek to change the Galatians' thinking regarding the "promise" and their status as heirs of Christ?

Use your review time to talk about the above questions and others that group members may raise. Let members lead the discussion wherever possible. To prepare for this review, spend some extra time in study to familiarize yourself with the basic outline of Galatians. Pray for clarity and sensitivity as you seek to help your group understand and apply Paul's message of salvation by grace.

Discovering Our Stories

a. Paul writes that the "new creation" is what counts. This is a new life of love in Christ, and the firstfruits of God's kingdom. What would our communities or world look like if ruled by the fruit of the Holy Spirit? How can your life, or your faith community, be a signpost of the new creation?

- *What might be one way God is prompting you to show his new creation this week by his Holy Spirit?*

b. What would it look like to boast in the cross of our Lord Jesus Christ in your life?

c. What is your next step as a result of this study?

d. Read Psalm 116 as a song of the redeemed, and as a boast in him.

More to Discover

Question 2c | 2 Corinthians 5:17; Revelation 21:4-5 (new creation)
2e | Philippians 3:3 (Israel of God)
3a | Acts 14:19; 2 Corinthians 11:24-25 (marks of Jesus)

9 Truly Free!

Optional Share Question

When you have free time, what do you like to do? What do you like to be free to do?

Getting Started

The good news in Galatians can be summed up in one phrase: "It is for freedom that Christ has set us free." In this lesson, we will look at some of the most important passages around freedom throughout Galatians. This is not just a review, but will help us grow in freedom.

Additional Note to the Leader: The power of the law is overwhelming. Believers and unbelievers alike often try to find peace with God by obeying rules. This always fails. As a result, they are caught in a net of guilt, frustration, and hopelessness.

People need to see that there is a way out of their guilt – a way of complete freedom and forgiveness in Christ. And those who already know that need to see that they have already been set free – no matter how much Satan, their accuser, tries to paralyze them with guilt and failure.

Many people still cling to rules and regulations as the only real way to become or stay right with God. The world says, prove yourself, measure up. Some people see Christianity as simply another set of do's and don'ts. And, knowing their inability to "live clean," they shake their heads and walk away, deciding that this kind of religion isn't for them. Even Christians may be very unaware of how much this do-and-don't mindset has crept into their approach to God.

Have you, as a leader, found true freedom in Christ? Do you know the exhilaration of actually being completely free of the law's demands and judgments? Can you say with Paul, "I am led by the Spirit; I am not under law"? Or do you find, as the Galatians were, that you need to rely at least a little on your own obedience to be found right before God?

As you prepare to lead this lesson, ask God to speak to your own heart about freedom in Christ. As you experience this miraculous truth and put it into practice in your own life you will be able to speak with conviction to your group members.

Discovering Together

1. Galatians 1:1-5
a. What do these verses tell us about Jesus?

b. What new things have you learned about Jesus in your study of Galatians?

- *What things in this passage might attract us to Jesus?*
- *What does Jesus have to offer?*
- *What might it mean to be "rescued from this present evil age"? What things today threaten to destroy our spiritual health and well-being? How does Jesus have the power to rescue us from this?*
- *In what ways does he offer us grace and peace?*
- *If you have been a Christian for a long time, what was the first thing that made you love Jesus? How can you refresh that?*
- *If you are a new believer, what drew you to Christ at this time in your life?*

Use these questions to focus first of all on Jesus. Theological questions and issues are only words unless they bring us to the one who loves us and gave his life for us.

Paul tells us a number of things about Jesus in these opening verses: Jesus sent Paul as an apostle; gave himself for our sins; died to rescue us from the present evil age; was raised from the dead; and now offers us grace and peace. Point your group to the one who can give freedom, forgiveness, and purpose in this world of confusion, guilt, and emptiness. Invite their comments and reflections on who Jesus is, but also offer your own personal experiences of getting to know Jesus.

2. Galatians 2:15-21
a. What do you think the word justified means in relationship to God?

- *How are we not justified, according to these verses?*

- *What is the only way to be justified?*
- *What are ways that people might try to become right with God? What do these verses say about those attempts?*
- *What would it be like to be justified in God's eyes? How does that happen? Do you want that? Would you like to put your faith in Christ? What questions do you still have?*
- *If you are a Christian, what were previous ways you tried to reach up to God? What words, images, or colors would you use to describe that? What words would you use to describe your freedom and standing before God now?*

God rescues us from his own just judgment by sending his Son to pay for our sin. We are justified through Christ's death on our behalf. You have already touched on this question in lesson 2. But these ideas are important enough to repeat over and over again, until the answers reach not only your group members' minds but their hearts as well. Also, you might now encourage your group members to make their responses more personal by adapting some of the questions above.

You probably know, from your discussions in past lessons, how close each member is to trusting Christ. So depend on the Spirit's leading, as always. Do not pressure anyone who is not ready, but do draw out thoughts and desires that are waiting to be expressed. Share freely also from your own experiences of trying to be justified by your own efforts – and the peace that you have found in Christ.

b. What does it mean to "live by faith in the Son of God"?

- *How might Galatians 5:6 give us another picture of this?*
- *Why is the desire to justify ourselves by our own good behavior so strong?*
- *What do we give up control of when we put our faith in Christ, according to these verses?*
- *What do we realize that we are powerless to do?*
- *How might pride or a desire for control hinder our putting our faith in Christ?*
- *If you are a Christian now, what does this look like in your life? How does it shape your daily life?*

It may help your group members to think of faith as strong trust, handing the reins of control over to someone else. When Jesus is our life, it will look like Galatians 5:6, a life of love. Listen carefully to discover if these things are standing in the way of your group members' faith in Christ.

3. Galatians 3:21-25
a. What have we learned from our failure under the law?

- *Who has kept this law perfectly? How many times a day might we break it?*
- *Even if we were highly motivated and determined, could we live a perfect life from now until we die? Why not? What does that teach us about ourselves?*

We have learned that we are unable to keep God's law perfectly. Perhaps look at Jesus' summary of the law in Matthew 22:37-40. Be aware that some in your group may be angry about any mention of a "law" or may view God as a real spoil-sport who just wants to make people feel guilty. They may think this set of rules is very archaic and has nothing to do with life today. Ask questions to probe their thinking:

- *Why might parents, employers, or governments have rules?*
- *Why do you think God set up these rules? What happens when people do not obey them? What results when people seek to comply with them?*
- *How might giving of the law show a shepherd's heart to guide and help? A father's heart to protect?*

Your discussion should again emphasize the role of the law as teacher: We would never know the extent of our sinful nature unless the law were there to show us how far short we fall from God's standard for our lives. Recall your discussion from lesson 4, which refers to the law as a kind of trusted old slave or governess who watches over us. Do not be afraid to help them face the reality of sin's power in human life. Take this opportunity to make these questions more personal to your group members:

- *What might it be like to feel the pressure of the law? How do you relate to that?*
- *How do you relate to the words "held prisoner," "locked up," and "prisoners of sin"?*
- *For Christians, what might be warning signs we are slipping under law again?*

b. To whom does the law lead us? Why?

- Do we have a choice in giving over the reins of control in our life? What is the alternative? In what way are we powerless?
- If you are a Christian, what was it like to find Christ? How did he meet you? How did that shift your perspective from do's and don'ts to faith in him?

Remind them, however, of the way of looking at faith discussed earlier: giving over the reins of control to someone else – in this case, Jesus Christ. You might share Romans 5:6-8 and 8:1-3 at this point (in the "More to Discover" so that all group members have access). So the law must lead us to Christ; it is powerless in itself to set us free from sin and death. Your discussion here should lead right into the next section.

---

4. Galatians 3:10-14
a. What did Christ do for you?

b. Why was this necessary?

- What can you receive as a result?
- What is the condition of every human being on this earth? According to the law, what should be done with us? What has God done instead? Why might God have done such a thing?
- What does verse 13 say? What could have motivated God to hang on a cross under a curse in our place?

You have already talked about the meaning of "justified," "righteous," "redeemed," "cursed," "Gentiles," and "hung on a tree" in lesson 3. Make sure that your group members understand these terms and can apply them personally. Move further than your initial discussion took you. Note the wording of the first question: "What did Christ do for you?" Encourage group members to answer these questions personally.

Discuss the enormity of what God has done for us. Galatians 2:20; Ephesians 3:17-19; 1 John 3:1; John 3:16 may be helpful verses.

If your group conversation leads to the "blessing of Abraham," do not neglect looking at Galatians 3:6.

- What blessing did Abraham receive as a result of his faith? Who else receives that blessing, according to verse 14? Is it possible *for anyone to receive the blessing of being called "righteous" by God? How?*

- *How do you celebrate that blessing?*

Abraham received righteousness; God declared him clean and sinless because of his faith. Remember in Genesis 15:6 it says Abraham believed and it was credited to him as righteousness; it is significant he was called righteous before he was circumcised. This supports Paul's point to the Galatians that circumcision does not justify you before God. Anyone who puts his or her faith in Christ will receive that same blessing of righteousness in God's eyes. But believers also receive "the promise of the Spirit." And this leads into the next passages from Galatians 4 and 5.

5. Galatians 4:4-7; 5:22-23

a. What can you receive through God's Son, according to Galatians 4:4-7?

- *What would you receive in exchange for giving up control of your attempts to "do it yourself"? What do you have to lose? What do you have to gain?*

The full benefits of God's offer in Christ Jesus are revealed clearly here for your group members: a close and loving Father/child relationship with God, and a Spirit-directed life filled with health, wholeness, and peace.

Are your group members ready to receive what God is longing to give them? Pray for the right words to speak as you make God's offer plain to them.

b. What fruit can come into your life through the Holy Spirit?

- *If you give your lives over to Christ and to the leading of the Holy Spirit, what rewards will you find? What kinds of things will you be free from?*
- *If you are a Christian, how have you seen that fruit in your life? How has it made a difference in your life, relationships with others, and relationship with God?*

As long as they are willing to give their lives over to Christ, and to obey God's will for them as they hear it in the Bible and in the Spirit's leading, their lives will be filled with love, joy, peace, patience, kindness, goodness, faithfulness, gentleness, and self-control. It is true that believers often choose to "gratify the desires of the sinful nature" and lose some of the spiritual fruits – even though they have not lost their standing as children of God.

6. Galatians 5:1a
a. Why did Christ set us free?

b. What do you think we can be set free from, through Christ?

- *What would you like to be set free from? How can you receive this freedom?*
- *Even if you are a Christian, are there still areas where you are drawn back to your own strength? to do's and don'ts? How can we pray for you and support you?*

This is the key question of the entire study of Galatians. Your group members, if they have not put their faith in Christ, are bound by the power of sin in their lives, by feelings of guilt and failure, by a broken relationship with God and with others. When they accept by faith what Christ has done for them, they step into freedom. You can help them take that step, through the working of the Holy Spirit in their lives.

This is such an important part of this lesson that you may wish to illustrate it visually. If so, bring to your session a number of lengths of rope, long enough to tie things. Before starting your discussion of this question, show the ropes and give several to each group member. Ask members to tie themselves up with these ropes. They will use some to tie their own feet or hands together; others they will use to tie themselves to each other.

When everyone is "tied up in knots," tell them that this is exactly the picture that Paul has drawn of the human condition. Sometimes we shackle ourselves with feelings of guilt, self-hatred, unworthiness, inadequacy. Sometimes this bondage is put on with someone else's help. Perhaps we are caught in a bitter, unforgiving relationship with someone. Perhaps we depend on someone else for our feelings of self-worth.

- *What does this exercise mean to you? How do you relate to it?*
- *How might this exercise show how we are not free to be who we are and called to do?*

All of this is the bondage of sin. It is from this bondage that Christ has come to set us free. God wants freedom for us! He wants the ropes untied. He wants our hands and feet and hearts loosed to live lives that are full of love, joy, peace, patience, kindness, goodness, gentleness, faithfulness, and self-control. He offers us all this in Christ.

If you do not have time or resources for this visual demonstration, at least ask your group members to imagine it with you.

Discovering Our Stories

a. **What is one thing from your study of Galatians that has impacted you most?**

b. **What have you implemented? How have your practices changed? What changes have you seen in your faith walk?**

c. **What did you learn about the process of Bible study?**

d. **Read Psalm 146 as a song of trust in God who frees, and not flesh (v. 7). He is worthy of our trust!**

More to Discover

Question 3a | Matthew 22:37-40 (summary of the law)

3b | Romans 5:6-8; 8:1-3 (law and Christ)

4a | Genesis 15:6 (blessing of Abraham)
   John 3:16; Galatians 2:20; Ephesians 3:17-19; 1 John 3:1 (what Christ did)

Invitation

Listen now to what God is saying to you.

You may be aware of things in your life that keep you from coming near to God. You may have thought of God as someone who is unsympathetic, angry, and punishing. You may feel as if you don't know how to pray or how to come near to God.

"But because of his great love for us, God, who is rich in mercy, made us alive with Christ even when we were dead in transgressions—it is by grace you have been saved" (Eph. 2:4-5). Jesus, God's Son, died on the cross to save us from our sins. It doesn't matter where you come from, what you've done in the past, or what your heritage is. God has been watching over you and caring for you, drawing you closer. "You also were included in Christ when you heard the message of truth, the gospel of your salvation" (Eph. 1:13).

Do you want to receive Jesus as your Savior and Lord? It's as simple as A-B-C:

- **Admit** that you have sinned and that you need God's forgiveness.
- **Believe** that God loves you and that Jesus has already paid the price for your sins.
- **Commit** your life to God in prayer, asking the Lord to forgive your sins, nurture you as his child, and fill you with the Holy Spirit.

Prayer of Commitment

Here is a prayer of commitment recognizing Jesus Christ as Savior. If you long to be in a loving relationship with Jesus, pray this prayer. If you have already committed your life to Jesus, use this prayer for renewal and praise.

> Dear God, I come to you simply and honestly to confess that I have sinned, that sin is a part of who I am. And yet I know that you listen to sinners who are truthful before you. So I come with empty hands and heart, asking for forgiveness.
>
> I confess that only through faith in Jesus Christ can I come to you. I confess my need for a Savior, and I thank you, Jesus, for dying on the cross to pay the price for my sins. Father, I ask that you forgive my sins and count me as righteous for Jesus' sake. Remove the guilt that accompanies my sin, and bring me into your presence.
>
> Holy Spirit of God, help me to pray, and teach me to live by your Word. Faithful God, help me to serve you faithfully. Make me more like Jesus each day, and help me to share with others the good news of your great salvation. In Jesus' name, Amen.

Bibliography

Barclay, William. *The Letters to the Galatians and Ephesians.* Philadelphia, PA: The Westminster Press, 1976.

Cole, R. Alan. *Galatians.* Tyndale New Testament Commentaries. Downers Grove, IL: IVP Academic, 2008.

Erdman, Charles. *The Epistle of Paul to the Galatians.* Grand Rapids, MI: Baker, 1984.

Mikolaski, S. J. "Galatians." In *The New Bible Commentary,* 3rd ed., edited by Donald Guthrie and J. A. Motyer. Grand Rapids, MI: Wm. B. Eerdmans Publishing Co., 1970.

Ryken, Philip Graham. *Galatians.* Reformed Expository Commentary. Philipsburg, NJ: P & R

Schreiner, Thomas R. *Galatians.* Zondervan Exegetical Commentary on the New Testament. Grand Rapids, MI: Zondervan, 2010.

Evaluation

discover Galatians

Please complete this evaluation. Your input is important. Send the evaluation to Attention: Discover Your Bible, 1700 28th Street SE, Grand Rapids, MI 49508. Or email your evaluation answers to info@discoveryourbible.org. Thank you.

1. Was this a home group ___ or a church-based ___ program?

2. Was the study used for

    ___ a community evangelism group?

    ___ a community faith-nurture group?

    ___ a church Bible study group?

3. How would you rate the materials?

    Study Guide: ☐ excellent ☐ very good ☐ good ☐ fair ☐ poor

    Leader Guide: ☐ excellent ☐ very good ☐ good ☐ fair ☐ poor

4. What were the strengths and weaknesses of the study?

5. What would you suggest to improve the material?

6. In general, what was the experience of your group?

7. Other comments

Your name (optional) _____

Address _____

DISCOVER YOUR BIBLE

**Thematic:
POWER OF
FORGIVENESS**

To explore similar studies, visit

GlobalCoffeeBreak.org

You can find samples and explore our Old and New Testament and thematic studies in English, Spanish, and Korean.

We are glad you enjoyed this study!

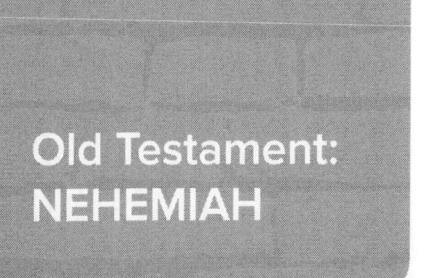

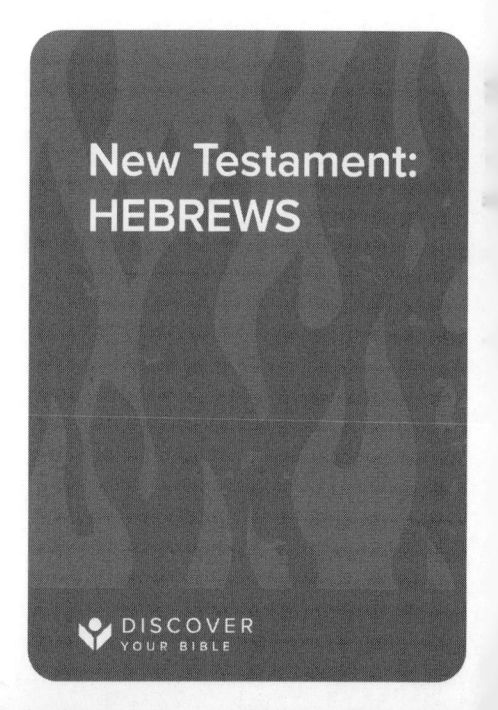

**New Testament:
HEBREWS**

**Old Testament:
NEHEMIAH**

DISCOVER YOUR BIBLE

GLOBAL COFFEE BREAK

A Global Coffee Break group is:

- Designed for dynamic group discussions
- Perfect for outreach
- Focused on the biblical text
- Geared for life change

Learn more about Global Coffee Break

GlobalCoffeeBreak.org